Beethoven's

NINE SYMPHONIES

Correlated with the

NINE SPIRITUAL MYSTERIES

———

By CORINNE HELINE

NEW AGE PRESS, INC.
3912 Wilshire Blvd.
Los Angeles, CA 90010

Second Edition, 1971

This is the volume
in a series of three
bearing the inclusive title
MUSIC – IT'S POWER AND MAGIC

Vol. I
MUSIC – THE KEYNOTE OF HUMAN EVOLUTION

Vol. II
THE COSMIC HARP

Vol. III
BEETHOVEN'S NINE SYMPHONIES
Correlated with the
NINE SPIRITUAL MYSTERIES

Beethoven's Nine Symphonies

BEETHOVEN THE MAN

Following is a description of Beethoven by a friend of the great composer as recorded by Ernest Newman in his volume entitled, *The Unconscious Beethoven:*

A group of friends were in a restaurant when Beethoven entered. A man of medium height with veritable Leonine head with gray mane and bright piercing eyes. He moved as in a dream and sat with dazed eyes. When spoken to he raised his eyelids like an eagle startled from its slumber and broke into a sad smile. Now and then from his coat he drew a book and began making notes. One day someone asked what he was writing: "He is composing, but he writes words not notes. Art has become a science with him and he knows what he can do. His imagination obeys his unfathomable reflection."

To an intimate, Beethoven once described his method of working: "I carry my ideas about with me for a long time before I write them down. My memory is so accurate that I am certain of not forgetting, even in the course of several years, a theme that comes to me. I alter it many times until I am satisfied, then begins in my head the working out of the broad, of the narrow, of the height, of the depth; and since I am conscious of what I want the fundamental idea never leaves me; it mounts, it grows. I see before my mind the picture in its whole extent, as it were in a single projection and nothing remains to be done but the work of writing it down. That gets along quickly according to the time I can spare for it, for I sometimes have several works in hand at once, but I never confuse one with another."

❊   ❊   ❊   ❊   ❊

"Beethoven was something more than a mere musician. He was a superman. . . . His wealth of ideas entitles him to a place beside Shakespeare and Michael Angelo in the history of the human spirit. . . . His symphonies are to him what the Sermon on the Mount is to the life of Jesus; his sonatas are the inner struggle of Jesus in the Garden of Gethsemane." — *Edmond Bordeaux* in LUDWIG VON BEETHOVEN

❋   ❋   ❋   ❋   ❋

"Beethoven was the Titan of the musical world. Other famous musicians may be compared one to another, but Beethoven brooks no comparison. He stands alone. He was the veritable Prometheus who was lifted up to bring down spiritual music from heaven — music that will enthrall and enchant mankind so long as the world stands. This was Beethoven." — *Ibid*

PROLOGUE

We stand today before the Beethoven Symphony as before the landmark of an entirely new period in the history of universal art, for through it there came into the world a phenomenon not even remotely approached by anything the art of any age or any people has to show us. — *Richard Wagner*

LUDWIG VON BEETHOVEN was born in Bonn, Germany, Dec. 16, 1770. He came to earth with a definite mission. To quote the words of Johan Herder in his philosophical studies of the *History of Mankind:* "God acts upon earth only by means of superior chosen men."

Beethoven was not born into a life of ease and happiness. Like most high souls, from early youth he was "a man of sorrows and acquainted with grief" for he was usually in desperate poverty and surrounded by uncongenial associates and environment. He said of himself: "I have no friend, I must live alone; but I know that in my heart God is nearer to me than to others. I approach him without fear, I have always known him. Neither am I anxious about my music, which no adverse fate can overtake, and which *will free him who understands it from the misery which afflicts others.*"

Beethoven's musical genius became evident at an early age. While yet a young man he was sent to Vienna where he studied for a time. He made his first appearance in that city in 1795, playing his own piano concerto in B-flat Major.

"In middle age," writes Charles O'Connell in the *Victor Book of the Symphony,* "in an age when republicanism was treason — he dared to be republican even while he commanded the support of courtiers and princes. When to be liberal was to be a heretic, he lived a large religion of humanism — without disrespect to established orthodoxy. When perfumed aristocrats eyed askance his stodgy figure, grotesque manners, absurd garb, he snarled and flashed and played the pettiness out of them. Too great to be ignored, too poor to be respected, too eccentric to be loved, he lived, one of the strangest figures in all history.

"Tragedy followed him like a hound. He became deaf and his last years were lived in a whirling void of silence. Silence! while from within he drew the sounds that all the world has loved to hear, and he of all the world should first have heard!"

In the dawn of civilization the Mysteries were founded for the purpose of teaching mankind how to enlarge his faculties and latent powers so he would be able to investigate the life and working of the higher astral, mental and spiritual vehicles belonging to man and the earth.

Many literary classics contain information relative to the Mysteries. This is true, for example, of Dante's *Divine Comedy,* and of Milton's *Paradise Lost and Regained.* Beethoven has musically described them in his nine great symphonies.

The path of Initiation leads to an investigation of the wonders and glories belonging to the inner realms of this earth planet. Man is much more than a physical body as seen by the physical eyes. He is composed of other subtler interpenetrating vehicles which also extend beyond the periphery of the physical body. So, too, is the earth composed of more than a physical globe. It has interpenetrating vehicles which extend far out into space. By means of Initiation man becomes aware of his finer bodies and their functions, and he acquires knowledge of the several vehicles of the earth planet and their functions.

During the nineteenth century a number of master souls took incarnation in order to bring again to mind various concepts of high spiritual truth concerned with Initiation — concepts which had long been cast aside and forgotten during the centuries of materialism that had enveloped the world. These truths were now to be revived for those who would accept them so that they might be strengthened and prepared for the strenuous and tragic years of the twentieth century.

Richard Wagner, another high musical Initiate, understood and appreciated something of Beethoven's great mission to the world. He perceived much of the sublime inner meaning and soul rapture of the Ninth Symphony. He considered it the supreme musical gift to mankind. When he built his beautiful shrine of music at Beyreuth he had its dedication commemorated by the immortal strains of Beethoven's celestial Ninth.

Berlioz has written concerning the Ninth Symphony: "Whatever may be said of this symphony it is certain that Beethoven, when finishing his work, and when contemplating the majestic dimensions of the monument he had just erected, might well have said to himself, 'Let death come now, my task is accomplished'."

The culmination of Beethoven's life work was reached in his nine symphonies. He began the first of these when the world stood upon the threshold of the nineteenth century. The first symphony was written in 1802. The ninth and last was completed and given to the world in 1824. With this sublime composition his earthly mission was approaching its glorious conclusion. His star call came in 1827.

In their highest aspect, Beethoven's Nine Symphonies are a musical interpretation of initiatory steps known as the Nine Spiritual Mysteries. The first, third, fifth and seventh symphonies are powerful, vigorous and commanding, typifying masculine characteristics centered in the head, or the intellect. The second, fourth, sixth and eighth symphonies are gentle, gracious, tender and beautiful, typifying the feminine characteristics centered in the heart, or the intuition. As an aspirant passes through the various initiatory steps of the Mysteries he learns to balance the forces of head and heart. Their union is known as the Mystic Marriage. It is this beautiful rite that Beethoven describes in the sublime music of the Ninth Symphony.

Each Initiation is accompanied by celestial music — music which Beethoven brought down to earth and translated for human hearing in the Nine Symphonies. When one reaches the exalted place of the Ninth Initiation he attains to the highest phase of mastership. He becomes an Adept. Then it is that he is found worthy to stand in the presence of the Lord Christ and receive His supreme benediction.

LUDWIG VAN BEETHOVEN

TABLE OF CONTENTS

Chapter I

FIRST SYMPHONY IN C MAJOR

It is acknowledged on every hand that in Beethoven the greatest and mightiest form of instrumental music found its greatest and mightiest exponent. — E. Markham Lee in *The Story of Symphonies.*

THE FIRST of the Nine Symphonies had its premiere in Vienna under Beethoven's own direction, April 2, 1800. This was the first of the mighty immortal series which is music's most colossal monument of this age. The year in which it was first produced suggested that it was the instrumental swan song of the 18th century.

The definite mission of Beethoven was to serve as a messenger of cosmic music. It was his destiny to reach out beyond the surface of this plane, and bring to mankind the glorious music of outer space, and this mission attained fulfillment in his Nine Symphonies. In these compositions Beethoven, in the words of Mr. Lee in his work quoted above, "reserves some of his largest and most weighty utterances. The outlook," he goes on to say, "is almost invariably big; the whole method of conception is one of grandeur and of Titanic force. He approaches the matter with serious mien and the outcome is serenely great."

The spiritual keynote of the First Symphony is *power.* The number one is indicated by an upright column, the first symbol of Diety as worshipped by primitive man in the earliest dawn of civilization. The number one also signifies the ego, the individual, the purpose of whose journey through evolution is to manifest his innate divinity.

True to symphonic form, this symphony is divided into four movements. An Allegro, which is preceded by an introductory Adagio expressing power, keynotes the composition. The second movement, an Andante, and the third, a Minuetto that is more

15

nearly a Scherzo, sustain an underlying assurance of an allegiance to this all-pervading but latent power. The Finale, in a spirit of exaltation, comes to a climax in a vast up-sweep of triumphant chords: "And God created heaven and earth and all that therein is; He saw His work, that it was good."

The First Symphony is a harbinger of the beauties and glories of the Nine Degrees of Initiation by which man becomes super-man and godman. In it Beethoven rises to heights and descends to depths in a way that few of his time could foresee or understand. Whoever comes to perceive the values incorporated in the inner structure of this symphony will place it among the finest inspirations of this magnificent musical genius.

Beethoven's compositions fall into definitely conceived patterns. This great musician did nothing without clear purpose. Thus, for instance, it is not to be taken as accidental that the introduction to the First Symphony is made up of twelve bars, each of which one may take as opening the door to one of the twelve zodiacal signs whose forces were all to play their part in the music truly cosmic in its expansion and nature. The twelve bars are divisible into three phases of four bars each, each of the four heralding the strain which is to follow. The four form an amalgamation of the powers that flow through the four elements of nature, namely: Fire, Air, Earth and Water.

The introductory Adagio, as noted above, consists of twelve bars in length, opening in the Key of F and leading into C Major, both of which have rich tonal power. In contrast, the second theme expresses the feminine attributes of gentleness and sweetness by bringing into play the alternate blending voices of the woodwinds.

The Minuet, harbinger of the Scherzo, is in rapid tempo. Here, writes a musical critic, "he rides freely on divine whims of modulation in a way which disturbed orthodox musicians of 1800."

The Finale is introduced by three bars in which the first violins reveal the ascending scale of the theme, bit by bit. The key progressions and swift passages all presage the coming to an end of the Old Age and the questing for the beginnings of the New.

In the third movement the music recapitulates the work of the two preceding movements in a quickened tempo that represents jubilance of spiritual attainment. This movement contains 353 bars, the numerical value of which is eleven, the number of perfect polarity. Both the Minuet and Trio Sections are in C.

In the Finale, which is described as a rondo, the numerical accent falls on eight, the number of wisdom. "The first subject cadences in the dominant within eight bars, and is followed by a motif accompanying another eight bars leading to a full tonic close."

This movement centers in a dialogue between the woodwinds and the strings, typifying the senses purified, the mind spiritualized. Trumpets and drums add fusing forces of the entire man. Here the three-eight-seven which equals eighteen or nine, indicates the foundations for the Great Work.

The phrasing of the Allegro is formed of four bars and is divided into two-plus-two which accents the fundamental principles of Polarity upon which all creation is based and which forms the cornerstone of all initiatory teachings. Beethoven here outlines cosmic principles or gives a blueprint of the universe as taught in musical Schools of Initiation, which like all ancient Mystery Temples, including those of early Masonry, included in their curriculum mathematics and astronomy along with music. The Allegro consists of 288 bars, 288 giving the numerical value of nine which is the number of man and of Initiation.

The second movement consists of 250 bars, the numerical value of which is seven, a number fundamental in human evolution. It keynotes the movement which is introduced in an unusual seven-bar metre. Later there is a return to the four-bar measures after which is employed a single bar to confirm the beginnings of individualization.

Beethoven introduces in this movement an independent solo part for the drums. He is telling us here that man must learn to reflect spirit in action. This fact is produced by the main theme being first divided between the upper and lower strings, typifying the path between the lower and higher natures. Later, the main theme is again repeated between the full strings and the woodwinds, thus outlining the musical path of transmutation by which desire is transmuted into spirit.

THE FIRST MYSTERY

Initiation into the Mysteries enables a person, when clad in his finer and more tenuous bodies, to enter and study the many wonderful truths which are concealed in the higher and finer envelopes of the earth.

In the First Mystery the candidate penetrates into the inner physical realms of the earth. The forces and activities that manifest in these inner earth realms, of which there are nine distinct strata, correlate with one of the Nine Spiritual Mysteries. In each of these nine Mysteries the candidate is taught to study these various activities and to work with these powerful inner-plane forces.

When mankind becomes sufficiently clairvoyant to be able to investigate these inner planes an astonishing new world will be revealed to him and geology will be one of the most fascinating of all the material sciences. This latter expression is a misnomer for in reality there is no such thing as a material science for when the heart of any science is fully revealed it becomes truly spiritual in its essential nature. As such it reveals God's love and care for this earth planet and all the evolving life waves that live upon it. The music of the Nine Symphonies when mystically interpreted open new vistas of idealism and understanding hitherto undreamed of.

The First Mystery is related to the physical earth. Within the Memory of Nature is concealed wondrous secrets relating to a long past evolutionary development of this earth planet. In the First Mystery one who is found worthy is taught to read in the Etheric Record and learn therefrom something of the wonders of the earth's past history. In that record he is able to see the vast green forests and the gigantic animals of Lemuria. The majestic redwoods of California are remnants of the Ancient Lemurian Period.

This epoch was followed by the silvery, mist-shrouded continent of Atlantis. Animal forms became smaller, the flora more variegated and delicate in color and texture. At the passing of Atlantis the present rainbow age was born, an age in which the Sun shines clear through an oxygenized atmosphere, and the present Aryan humanity, the Fifth Root Race, came into being.

The majesty of Beethoven's First Symphony is descriptive of tremendous earth transformation. In its four movements it is as though the composer were setting to music the creative fiats of God. The music mounts higher and higher, culminating in the soaring Finale that translates into immortal tone the pronouncement at the close of the six creative days as recorded in Genesis that everything that had been made was good, "was very good."

Chapter II

SECOND SYMPHONY IN D MAJOR

This symphony is music that breathes forth serenity, beauty, gaiety and courage. — *Philip Hale* in BOSTON SYMPHONY NOTES.

HE SECOND of the Nine Symphonies was first performed in Vienna, April 5, 1803. Its spiritual keynote is Love. Number two expresses the feminine or mother principle of God. This principle manifests as love supreme, the power which animates the entire Second Symphony, imparting to the music such beauty and tenderness that many devotees of Beethoven's symphonies have declared it to be the most beautiful of them all. The all-embracing protectiveness of the mother spirit broods over some of its movements. In others the spirit of sacrifice, inseparable from mother love, finds expression in certain tender strains. The Scherzo breathes forth happiness so refined and distilled that it is like a waft of perfumed air. It has the effect of uplifting and refreshing a drooping spirit.

Beethoven's increasing deafness served to shut out physical distractions so that he might the more clearly capture the celestial harmonies that are ever playing throughout our ordered cosmos.

The tonal quality of the Second Symphony is filled with orchestral colors that impart to its music a quality of clarity and luminosity from its opening measures to the close.

The first movement produces the effect of brilliant sunshine. The Larghetto sounds in subdued colors like the varied play of light and shadow on some clear surface. The Scherzo flashes and sparkles in vivacious gaiety and beauty, bursting into dynamic contrasts in the Finale.

Beneath its delicately appealing melody and general tone of brightness this symphony is full of "daring episodes" with other-world intimations and faint echoings that puzzled and confused critics of the time.

This movement with its sudden bursts of chords and capricous modulations were often severely criticized by reviewers of Beethoven's time, but there were also those who recognized its tonal effects as truly magnificent. Beethoven ever worked within the framework of illimitable spaces.

Berlioz, in his commentary on this symphony, asserts that the Andante "is a pure and frank song . . . whose character is never far removed from the sentiment of tenderness which forms the distinctive character of a principal idea. It is a ravishing picture," he continues, "of innocent pleasure which is scarcely shadowed by a few melancholy accents." Berlioz then describes the Scherzo as "frankly gay in its fantastic capriciousness as the Andante has been wholly and serenely happy; for this symphony is smiling throughout; the war-like bursts of the first Allegro are wholly free from violence; there is only the youthful ardor of a noble heart in which the most beautiful illusions of life are preserved untainted. The composer still believes in immortal glory, in love, in devotion. What abandon in his gaiety. . . . It is as though you were watching the fairy sports of Oberon's graceful spirits."

"The Finale," he adds "is of like nature. . . . A second Scherzo in two-time, and its playfulness has perhaps something still more delicate, more piquant."

After one of the earliest performances of this symphony in Leipsic in 1804, a critic of more than contemporary discernment averred that it was a composition of such fine, such rich ideas that the work would live and that it would "always be heard with renewed pleasure when a thousand things that are today in fashion will have been buried."

Since this symphony was written under external circumstances that were of a depressing nature due to physical ailments from which the composer suffered and the "crushing news" that Guilietta Guicciardi, a pupil of his with whom he had fallen in love, had married Count Gallenberg, critics have not failed to comment on the contradiction between the personal melancholy mood of the composer at the time and the joyous, lovable music he wrought in his Second Symphony.

The answer to the question posed by this circumstance is usually disposed of after the manner of a commentator who concluded that "in view of the tragedy of that summer, this symphony might, perhaps, best be looked upon as an escape."

If Beethoven had lived to personal ends such an explanation would in all probability be completely true. But Beethoven lived to serve universal, impersonal ends. He had dedicated his life to bring to humanity the healing, redeeming powers of beauty through the most exalted of all the arts, the art of music. Beethoven was a titanic ego functioning within the limitations of a personal form. When he gave himself to bring down from the heaven world his inspired musical communications his consciousness ascended to levels where the purely personal is lost in the universal. Hence we conclude on the basis of Beethoven's character, and the purpose that animated his life and his dedication to serve spiritual purpose, that when, as in the case of composing the Second Symphony the joy and love it radiates is not the result of a desperate effort of the will to escape from his personal trial and tribulation but rather a surrender of his personal concerns, be they either of a mournful or of a joyously exultant nature, to the impersonal transmission of which the heavenly world of tone was capable of imparting to man through an ego qualified to serve in so exalted a capacity.

Marion M. Scott, in *Master Musicians Series* observes, relative to the composition of the Second Symphony, that while Beethoven was walking in the meadows of Heiligenstadt, his mind had roamed the Elysian Fields. In other words, while his person was walking here below, his higher self was soaring far above. It was then that he saw, in the words of Marion Scott, "as sometimes happens in mountain ranges, across the near gulf and intervening ranges, a radiant vision of distant mountains on the horizon — he had seen Joy." That vision he left us in the Second Symphony.

As previously noted, the principal theme of the Second Symphony is Love. From Love springs confidence, serenity, joy and that great peace that passeth understanding. All of these

qualities are beautifully expressed throughout the symphony
which concludes on the triumphant note that spirit is supreme
and that it is possible for the spirit to remain unfettered and
untouched by all the inharmonies and disillusionments of the
outside world. Emerson expressed it most aptly when he wrote:
"It is only the finite that has wrought and suffered; the Infinite
lies stretched in smiling repose." This is the inspiring message
of the Second Symphony.

THE SECOND MYSTERY

The Second Mystery is connected with the second earth
sheath called the Fluidic Layer. In this sheath are reflected the
harmonious, pulsating forces of the etheric realm. The work of
this Mystery has much to do with the secret of the ethers,
including the beings who inhabit this realm. These include the
nature spirits that do so much to beautify the earth. The etheric
realm transcends the sphere of darkness and death. Here one
moves in perpetual light and in a realm of a life immortal.

There are four ethers with which man is concerned. The two
lower ethers relate to his life on the physical plane; the more
earthy its character, the denser are these two lower ethers. The
two higher ethers relate to man's aesthetic and spiritual activities.
They have to do with his higher faculties. Hence the more
sensitized his nature, the more it is oriented toward spiritual
unfoldment and the more rapid is his advancement on the path.

St. Paul referred to man's body as the temple of the living
God. The two pillars supporting this temple are the two nervous
systems, the cerebro-spinal and the sympathetic. These two
systems are directly related to the Mysteries. It is said that in
these chaotic and uncertain times the great majority of humanity
is affected to some extent with nervous mal-adjustments. This is
because man has not learned to rightly adapt his life and
activities to the inflow and outflow of the etheric forces. When
he understands these inner forces and lives more in harmony
with the laws governing the etheric realms he will become
sensitive and responsive to this subtle and beautiful influence.
The human body of the future will differ greatly from that of

today. It will possess faculties of such a high order as are scarcely dreamed of at present.

This movement with its sudden bursts of chords and capricious of the angelic Hierarchy which is expert in the manipulation of the etheric forces. The Angels who minister to the earth contact it through the etheric realm. Although they are present in surrounding space their presence is not recognized because of a lack of etheric sight. This higher octave of vision will become quite general in the course of the Aquarian Age. A wonderful companionship and brotherhood will then be established between the human and the angelic kingdoms.

In the tender beauty and the fairy-like delicacy, the sweetness and purity of many passages in his Second Symphony, Beethoven is describing something of the loveliness of this realm and the beauty and light of these angelic beings who inhabit it.

To again quote from Mr. Scott, "There was in Beethoven something that transcended the ethics of Aeschylus and Sophocles — something that set him beside blind Homer and Virgil whose high thoughts reflected "the radiance of some mysterious and unrisen day." Like them he could pass through tragedy to the greater knowledge beyond, where birth and death, joy and sorrow, are but different sides of the same gold coin of life minted by God in eternity.

The high spiritual power of the Mysteries increases with each ascending degree. In the glorious music of the Second Symphony there sounds an echoing and re-echoing of that spiritual force which will only attain its perfection and final summation in the celestial music of the Ninth Symphony.

Beethoven drew inspiration from the mountains during the time he worked on the Second Symphony. The towering peaks on which he ofttimes gazed with rapture might well be regarded as a physical reflection of the high spiritual realm into which his spirit was caught up in ecstatic joy as he endeavored to transcribe in music the lofty spiritual meaning of the Mysteries.

In the Second Mystery one passes into the etheric realm, therein to study the mysteries of flowers and plants and the ministry of Angels in connection with them. The exquisite sweetness of the Second Symphony is redolent with these rare secrets.

With the approaching New Age man will become increasingly clairvoyant. This will reveal a fascinating new world. Man will be able to observe the life and activities of the nature spirits and also that of the angelic messengers who direct and supervise their activities throughout the entire plant kingdom. As a result of this development botany will become one of the most interesting of all sciences.

One of the most fascinating aspects of New Age botany will be experimentation dealing with the effects of concentrated human thought upon the life and growth of the plant kingdom. Some important experiments along this line are now being conducted in this country and notably in India. Their results are certain to be vastly important and more far reaching than can be foreseen at this time. It will mean expanded boundaries in terms of man's consciousness, an enlargement of his sphere of life.

Chapter III

THE THIRD SYMPHONY IN E FLAT MAJOR (EROICA)

Beethoven's heart was filled with divine fire and it knew no boundary; all heaven and earth were his fields of exploration where he loved, dreamed, suffered greatly, and poured his feelings into his art. In whiteheat he transformed all that he touched, making it luminous with divine fire.

"At Vienna I heard for the first time one of his symphonies, the *Eroica*. Henceforth I had but one idea: to make the acquaintance of this great genius, to see him, if only once." — *Rossini*

"Its glorious themes and the superb beauty of its musical thought allow it to remain, more than a hundred years after its composition, as one of the masterpieces of musical creativeness." — *E. Markham Lee*.

"The music of the *Eroica* is profound, magnificently illustrative of an idealistic heroism. It typifies the pure spirit of heroism idealized and universalized. The First Movement expresses the heroism of intrepidity wherein faith becomes the great transforming power that purifies and exalts. The Funeral March contains no representation of death as such but lifts and exalts and proclaims the powers of Life Eternal. For the wide sweep of Beethoven's concept contained no shadowing of death.

"The Scherzo expresses and maintains this confidence and serenity while the Finale is aspiring and joyous with all the conscious knowing of the great musical seer, a shining foreshadowing of the sunshine forces later to be released in the inspiring measures of the Ninth Symphony." — *John N. Burk* in LIFE AND WORKS OF BEETHOVEN.

HE THIRD of the Nine Symphonies was begun in 1803 and completed in the following year. It was first performed in Vienna in 1805.

The spiritual keynote of the Third Symphony is Strength. The number three is formed by uniting one (power) and two (love). From the union of power and love is born the third attribute, Strength. It is this soul power of strength which becomes the underlying theme of Beethoven's Third.

The true greatness of Beethoven began to manifest in this stupendous work. Here is music of concentrated and dynamic

26

force. Its conception is so vast that the pen was unable to keep pace with the cosmic scheme as it was revealed to him in all its colossal proportions. Every bar bears a heroic stamp. This is not conventional music but a transcription of heavenly strains that, like an unbroken melody, moves in long currents of ebb and flow, a mighty symphony in which the currents of life and death, or life transcendent, vie with each other in measure after measure in supernal glory.

All critics concur on the spirit of universality which permeates this Symphony. The tonal magic ascends mountain peaks and descends into subterranean valleys suffusing all the earth with effulgent light. The recapitulation restates the themes in a tempo of ever increasing strength and beauty.

The Third Symphony was especially close to Beethoven's heart. Many who knew him intimately have stated that this symphony, the *Eroica*, was his favorite. Most commentators have associated this symphony with special political significance. However, it is the deeper or esoteric aspects in which we are primarily interested.

This symphony, like all of Beethoven's Nine, is divided into four parts, designated in this composition as Allegro, Funeral March, Scherzo and Finale.

The nature and sequence of the four parts have occasioned many and varied speculations as to just what the composer had in mind when creating the symphony. The gay Scherzo which follows the Funeral March has proven especially perplexing to commentators. But, in the words of Robert Bagar and Louis Biancolli in the *Concert Companion* "the musicologist, the historian, and the fictionist may be permitted their interpretations, but the music remains as a monument to a great and powerfully expressive mind, whose thoughts and imaginings, whatever they may have been, became crystallized into the brilliant, overwhelming pattern of a timeless creation."

As for what some have felt to be the inappropriativeness of the gay Scherzo following immediately after the Funeral March, this presents no difficulty of interpretation in the light of the soul's deeper experience. When an aspirant embarks earnestly on the path of transmuting the lower nature into the higher, the experiences encountered are often fraught with failures and frustrations, with pain and sorrow. Many times it is then that their sounds in the seeker's heart, the solemn and mournful tones of the funeral march of renunciation of the lesser self. With the attainment of this new-found soul strength, however, the renewed, refreshed spirit sings of its gladness and delight as expressed in the Scherzo. In the words of David, the sweet singer of Israel, "Sorrow endureth for the night but joy cometh in the morning."

The musical Initiate, Richard Wagner, has expressed the inner and deeper values embodied in this symphony with such spiritual insight that we quote from it at some length. In his inspired words, the first movement "is to be taken in its widest sense, and in no wise to be conceived as relating merely to a military hero. If we broadly connote by "hero" ("held") the whole, the full-fledged *man*, in whom are present all the purely human feelings of love, of grief, of force, in their highest fill and strength, then we shall rightly grasp the subject which the artist lets appeal to us in the speaking accents of his tone-work. The artistic space of this work is filled with all the varied, increasing feelings of a strong, a consummate individuality, to which nothing human is a stranger but which includes within itself all truly human, and utters it in such a fashion that, after frankly manifesting every noble passion, it teaches a final rounding of its nature, wherein the most feeling softness is wedded with the most energetic force. The heroic tendency of this art work is the progress towards that rounding off."

For Wagner the first movement "embraces, as in a glowing furnace, all the emotions of a richly gifted nature in the heyday of unresting youth, yet all these feelings spring from one main faculty and that is *Force*. . . . We see a Titan wrestling with the gods."

Of the second movement with its "shattering force, which reaches the tragic crisis, the tone-poet clothes its proclamation in the musical apparel of a Funeral March. Emotion tamed by deep grief, moving in solemn sorrow, tells us its tale in stirring tones."

Romaine Rolland considered the Funeral March "one of the

grandest things in music. It is a pageant," he observes, "of world tribulations rather than an elegy for Napoleon," and Pitts Sanborn called it "one of the most tremendous lamentations conceived in any art."

Of the third movement Wagner has this to say: "Force robbed of its destructive arrogance — by the chastening of its deep sorrow — the third movement shows in all its buoyant gaiety. Its wild unruliness has shaped itself to fresh, to blithe activity; we have before us now this lovable, glad man, who passes hale and hearty through the fields of Nature." This was Beethoven's first Scherzo, and is regarded by many as among his greatest.

In the Finale tremendous measures of exultant strength are released proclaiming the achievement of self-mastery. It is music wherein every physical atom becomes attuned to the music of the spheres.

As understood by Wagner, the Finale depicts the whole man, that is, the "deeply, stoutly suffering man" and the "gladly, blithely doing man," the two harmoniously "at one with self, in these emotions where the memory of sorrow becomes itself the shaping force of noble deeds."

For the foregoing Wagnerian quotes we are indebted to Laurence Gilman's *Stories of Symphonic Music*.

Human language can at best convey only very haltingly the spiritual essence and significance of art works that spring from a consciousness capable of tuning in with the higher spiritual planes through a personality that possesses the rare ability to transcribe them to an unmistakable degree for human hearing. That Wagner had the perception to recognize inner values in Beethoven's Third Symphony more fully and clearly than most mortals, is amply demonstrated in the esotericism that forms the inner structure of all his immortal works. Hence that which he has to say about Beethoven's Third holds more than a surface meaning, more than comes within grasp by a mere casual hearing.

For example, when Wagner speaks of the Finale as summing up the symphony's presentation of man's sorrows and struggles as finally blended harmoniously into his joyous creative experiences, and from which springs an art form possessing "force for noble deeds," he is holding with Pythagoras, who gave to three

the attribute of harmony, and also affirming the truth of the
the experiences encountered are often fraught with failures and
symbolism of Masonry's three supporting pillars of wisdom,
strength and beauty.

More than this, Wagner speaks of the Finale of the Third
as depicting "the whole man," the "total Man, who shouts to us
the avowal of his Godhood."

Consider this statement in relation to the vibratory field of
three within which the Third Symphony takes form. Everywhere
among the ancients the number three was deemed the most
sacred of numbers. There is no symbol more important than the
equilateral triangle used as the symbol of Deity. Plato saw in
it the image of the Supreme Being, and according to Aristotle
the number three contains within itself a beginning and an end.
It was in the Trinity which Plato identified with the Supreme
Being that man was created, or, in the words of Wagner, "the
whole, the total man, the man who shouts to us the avowal of
his Godhood." In this brief commentary of Wagner's we have
an arresting instance of one musical Initiate interpreting what
another of corresponding elevation of creativeness has set down
for the hearing of less perceiving ears.

Of the Third Symphony Pitts Sanborn has this to say: "The
Third embodies the developments with which Beethoven revolu-
tionized the symphony. In amplitude and opulence no previous
symphonic movement had ever equalled or even approached
the initial Allegro con brio, and it may be doubted whether any
has subsequently surpassed it. Sensitive listeners hearing it
for the first time may well have cried out with Miranda: "O
brave new world!"

The supreme struggle that confronts every human being is
the conquest of the personality by the powers of spirit. This is
a battle in which every ego is engaged many times in every life
cycle and when the victory is finally consummated the spirit
rises free, emancipated, victorious. It is this conflict and victory
that Beethoven has portrayed so magnificently in his *Eroica*.
It is undoubtedly for this reason that Beethoven asserted that
this composition was his favorite symphony.

THE THIRD MYSTERY

The Third Mystery is connected with the third sheath of the earth which is known as the Vapor Layer. Into this stratum is reflected the astral or desire world. Here one comes to understand as never before the close relationship between man and the planet upon which he lives. He comes to understand how his own unbridled desire nature influences and releases certain sinister forces within the corresponding layer in the earth. He also realizes how the control of the desires within himself tend to impede the operation of the destructive forces within the body of the earth. For example, if mankind en masse had complete mastery over the desire nature within itself, there would be less devastation from fires, floods, cyclones, volcanic eruptions and other violent upheavals of nature. This may on first thought seem strange and unbelievable to one who has not looked into the inner secrets of nature and of man. It was the complete control of the lower nature within three holy men described in the Book of Daniel that enabled them to remain unharmed in the "burning fiery furnace." For the same reason holy men in India, and elsewhere, are able to pass through forests unmolested by ferocious beasts and unhurt by poisonous reptiles. As one meditates upon these facts one comes to realize more fully the profound significance of the words of Solomon: "He that controlleth himself is greater than he that taketh a city." Richard Wagner expressed this same truth in his music-drama Parsifal, giving as its keynote, "Great is the strength of desire, but greater is the strength of overcoming." It is this power that forms the underlying theme of Beethoven's Third Symphony.

It is only one who has attained complete self-conquest such as Beethoven describes in the *Eroica* that can safely enter and investigate the desire realms of the earth.

In the Third Mystery the gorgeous colors of the astral world are reflected in the third, or Vapor Stratum of the earth, and it becomes a veritable rainbow of translucent beauty. Many of the colors herein reflected have never been seen on the physical plane for their vibratory frequencies are too high to be cognized by physical sight. Here the candidate learns to control the desire rhythms within his own body and to transform them into spiritual power. In the higher Mysteries he also learns how to control desire currents in the outer world as for instance, in certain vast assemblages where emotions tend to run high, as in a race riot, such an advanced one possesses the power to master these emotions and so avert disaster or tragedy.

Chapter IV

THE FOURTH SYMPHONY IN B FLAT MAJOR

The Fourth Symphony is like a "slender Greek maiden between two Norse giants." — *Robert Schumann*

THE FOURTH of the Nine Symphonies was composed in the summer of 1806. It was done midst the pleasantest surroundings and under conditions of inner and outer serenity. The symphony that then came into being is poetically referred to by Romaine Rolland as "a pure, fragrant flower which treasures up the perfume of those days."

It has been noted previously that the number three (strength) is a masculine emanation of the combined vibratory values of one (power) and two (love). The number four (beauty) is a feminine emanation which is formed by the blending of one (power), two (love) and three (strength). Thus there is an intimate relationship between strength and beauty. The two main columns at the entrance of King Solomon's Temple bear the signatures of strength and beauty. It is interesting to note that various writers on Beethoven's symphonies find a close relationship between the Third and the Fourth. The Third is centered in power and strength and the Fourth in love and beauty. "In his masculine moods," writes Alexander Wheelock Thayer, "Beethoven tips the mountain crests with celestial fire; in his feminine moods he fills the valleys with heavenly sweetness." This, the preeminently feminine Fourth he hears as the "symphony of dreaming."

In the development of pure soul strength, beauty is always latent in its heart, and the very essence of true spiritual beauty will always be found to possess a certain inner strength. The Fourth Symphony has also been referred to as the symphony of happiness and its four movements identified with the qualities of Serenity, Happiness, Beauty and Peace.

Considering the four parts, the introductory Adagio is charac-
terized by an angelic sweetness; it is possessed of a profound
and mystic serenity. "Its form is so pure and the effect of its
melody so angelic" writes Hector Berlioz, "and of such irresist-
ible tenderness that the prodigious art by which this perfection
is attained disappears completely. From the very first bars we
are overtaken by an emotion which toward the close becomes
so overpowering in its intensity that only among the giants of
poetic art can we find anything to compare with this sublime
page of the giant of music. Nothing indeed," he concludes,
"more resembles the impression produced by this Adagio than
that which we experience when we read the touching episode
of Francesca da Rimini in *Divina Commedia.*"

The second movement, an Adagio in E flat major, breathes a
fervor that yet again some commentators have sought to link
to the composer's personal love life. But here Berlioz, like
Wagner, perceives the true, lofty and impersonal source of
Beethoven's inspiration. "The being who wrote such a marvel of
inspiration as this movement" avers Berlioz, "is not a man. Such
must be the song of the Archangel Michael as he contemplates
the world's uprising to the threshold of the empyrean."

The third movement (Allegro vivace) invokes sheer delight.
It is bright and entrancing. There is happiness in the lilting
strings, in the wind instruments and the harmonic beat of the
drums. It is a veritable song of the beauty which the receptive
soul comes to realize as immortal in itself, having neither
beginning nor end. At this point one is moved to exclaim with
Wagner that it is music that cannot be grasped otherwise than
through "the idea of magic."

The Finale closes on "a gleaming vista wherein the harmony
of the seen and the unseen worlds meet and converse." It
breathes a sweet and tender benediction of peace. It is the peace
which comes only to the soul that has learned to transmute
life's difficulties and problems into pure soul beauty. The
highest meaning of the number four is this ability of the illumined
or Christed one to rise above the limitations of human life,
and slowly but surely change the rough Ashler into the
perfect Cube.

THE FOURTH MYSTERY

The Fourth Mystery is correlated to the fourth earth layer termed the Watery Stratum. Therein is reflected the forces of the mental sphere of the earth known as the realm of concrete thought. The Third Mystery has to do with the overcoming of the desire nature. The next step in attainment is the illuminating or the spiritualizing of the mind. This involves long and arduous processes and requires many lives for its complete consummation. For the average person the mind is held in thralldom to the personality. The life is centered largely in the "I," or the concerns of the personal life. As one enters upon the Path he learns to gradually disengage the mind from the personality and to link it with the spirit. It is then that the mind becomes a light, a light that brightens the world. The life and work of such a person bears the impress of immortality.

One of the most profound books in the Bible and one of the supreme initiatory legends in all world literature is the Book of Job. This is the story of the Great Overcoming. So long as the spirit is in bondage to the "three friends," the physical body, the desire nature and the concrete or material mind, the personality is subject to all the difficulties and limitations of the physical life such as poverty, disease and death.

The supreme transforming event in the life of Job was the appearance of Elihu. His coming represents the final victory of detaching the mind from the personality and its union with the spirit. This illumination or Christing of the mind is the accomplishment related to the Fourth Mystery and described musically in the Fourth Symphony. When Job arrived at this stage of spiritual unfoldment his physical well being was recovered, his worldly wealth regained in double measure and even the life of his children restored to him. Job was now, in the words of the poet, "the master of his fate, the captain of his soul." It was this same ideal which the Christian Initiate, St. Paul, gave to his disciples when he said, "Let that mind be in you which was also in Christ Jesus."

In the Fourth Mystery the forces of the World of Thought are reflected in the fourth earth stratum, known as the Watery

Stratum. This realm is not composed of water as we think of this element, but it is filled with a luminous silvery mist in which are reflected the archetypal patterns which lie behind all created things.

The World of Concrete Thought, known as the Second Heaven, is the home of all these archetypal patterns. It is here, between earth lives that the ego spends much time learning how to build the archetype which will be the pattern for his next earth body.

It is significant to note it is on the mental plane that these archetypal patterns are built, for this gives us a clearer concept of the tremendous power of creative thought. The candidate in the Fourth Mystery learns how to use the power of constructive and creative thinking and the realization that by this means he builds or mars his life. By the power of thought he may debase or glorify himself. Metaphysical movements like Christian Science, Unity and Divine Science are performing a most important service in the world today in taking for their fundamental teachings the power of constructive thinking. How true it is that thoughts are things. The Bible expresses this profound truth in the statement "As a man thinketh in his heart, so is he."

Chapter V

THE FIFTH SYMPHONY IN C MINOR

"The spirit of Beethoven is incarnate in his music, and he that hath heard the Fifth Symphony hath heard Beethoven." — *Sir Oliver Lodge*

THE FIFTH SYMPHONY is a song of the Four Elements — Fire, Air, Water and Earth. It is breath-taking in its intensity and power. The extreme sensitives of Beethoven's day are said to have been thrown into convulsions by its great out-sweeping tides of veritable cosmic fire.

This is how Wagner describes the "gigantic energy" of this symphony's first movement: "He (Beethoven) arrests the waves of the sea and lays bare the ground of the ocean, which stops the clouds in their courses, dispels the mist and reveals the pure blue sky and the burning face of the Sun himself."

In its four parts the Symphony sings the song of each Element. While each of these parts is separate and distinct from each other they are magically bound together by a golden thread of harmony. Critics have often remarked about the rythmic concord of the Four Elements.

The first movement (Allegro con brio) is keyed to the Element of Fire. The second movement (Andante con moto) is related to Air. It is the most irregular of the four movements. The third movement (Allegro) is closely linked to the first while in no way becoming a repetition of it. It conveys a mysterious shimmering, watery character. Then in the Finale it is as though the very body of the Earth reached forth in triumph to receive, unite and integrate this cosmic fourfold elemental power.

The Fifth Symphony was composed in late 1807 or early in 1808. Both the Fifth Symphony and its successor, the Sixth, were first performed in Vienna on December 22, 1808.

The spiritual keynote of the Fifth Symphony is **Freedom.**

Of all the nine great symphonies by Beethoven this one is probably the best known, the best understood and the most popular. It has been proclaimed "faultless in conception and flawless in construction . . . a lofty and enduring monument to the incomparable genius and executive ability of its author." It is music that soars above the personal and the transient in life; it bears no reference to the passing, external scene but bodies forth from cosmic levels a moral force designed to strengthen the inner being of all who hear it. It is pure, refined, abstract music aimed to stir the soul of man into remembrance of his divine, immortal nature and to draw on its powers to step up higher. And this indeed it does, whether there be conscious recognition of the fact or not. Here is a tonal structure raised to "cosmic utterance." It speaks redemptively to the inmost spirit of man because its sound patterns are so fully harmonious to both the activities of the Grand Man of the Universe and those within His reflection in the microcosmic man of earth.

Each of the four movements is by itself a brilliant creation. Taken altogether they constitute a work of imposing grandeur.

The first movement, Allegro con brio, opens with four unison notes which Beethoven once explained, sounded forth Fate's knocking at the door. The second movement, Andante con moto, carries a note of sadness, yet wonderfully beautiful, and is further enhanced by one of those majestic marching themes such as only Beethoven could conceive.

Considered together the first and second movements are a veritable outburst of will defiance which grows more vehement and intense until the resisting forces are beaten back and down. As one commentator expressed it, the first two movements are the song of a strong willed ego determined to break the bonds of fate or destiny and to rise above their limitations.

Fate, it is to be added, is but another name for the universal karmic law of cause and effect. It is not a cold, detached abstraction. It is an active, living power interwoven into the very fabric of life. As a man or nation sows, so must they also reap. Man, both individually and collectively, resents this truth before he is spiritually awakened. He refuses to accept the fact that his

sorrows and misfortunes are the result of his own misdeeds and
mistaken actions. The anger, bitterness, defiance and refutation
which the awakening soul endures is depicted in the first two
movements of the Fifth Symphony.

With the third movement a great transformation occurs.
Now the music becomes weirdly beautiful and filled with a
strange mysticism that portends vast deeps and inscrutable
heights, as yet unscaled and unexplored. Here gradually but
inevitably, as softly and beautifully as the opening petals of a
flower, the spirit is awakened more fully to the true purpose and
mystery of life. A new and deeper realization is born, but when
the laws of life are understood and harmoniously applied they
are found to be not evil, but good.

The third movement or Scherzo has some eloquent base
passages and its rhythmic tone figures are full of veiled mystery
and heavy with dark foreboding. It insinuates itself into the
"proud and fiery" Finale near the coda which is of amazing
brilliancy, ending with a Presto which fairly sweeps the hearer
away with it.

There is nothing more ethereally beautiful in all music than
the transition from the Scherzo to the Finale wherein this
realization is fully born within the awakened or illumined soul.
It is then with a song of rejoicing that the spirit stands free and
untrammeled for all time and eternity, never again to be held in
bondage to karmic law. The glory music of the Scherzo and the
Finale sound the triumphant song of one who has thus attained.
This high "freedom music" is the divine heritage of every soul
who thus learns to emancipate himself by passing from the
finiteness of personal living into the infinity of eternal being.

In the words of Charles O'Connell, "In the broad sense, this
is not the expression of one man's thought or feeling. This is the
utterance of a torn mental and puzzled and cynical and hopeful
— and finally triumphant humanity. This is the voice of the
people, of a world, pitiful and puny; yet bearing within it the
elements of final greatness . . . surely the Fifth has a more
powerful, direct and universal appeal to human nature than any
other great music in existence."

The Finale is of such magnificence and richness that in

comparison with it there are few pieces that could be played
without being completely crushed.

E. Markham Lee in *The Story of the Symphony* writes thus
of the Fifth: "Colossal in its majestic power, romantic in its
very essence, and titanic in its inherent ideas, the C minor
Symphony stands out as one of the noblest and most characteristic of Beethoven's works. Coming as it does in mid-path of
his Nine Symphonies, it is unlike its fellows on either side, and
by its nobility and majesty holds its proud head aloof with a
dignity which it is well able to sustain. Beethoven commenced
work upon it soon after the completion of the *Eroica,* and the
same deep seriousness and earnestness are apparent."

This powerful, magnificent, and at the same time terrific
music is describing the glorious freedom which only the spirit
can know that has broken the chain that binds it to the personality and has awakened to the raptures of pure unadulterated
spirit. This symphony is the sublime song of emanicipation. It
is a musical interpretation of man's epic struggle on soul levels.
It is an exultant song of triumph in which the emancipated one
breaks asunder the bonds of the finite and passes victoriously
and exultantly into the glorious freedom of the infinite.

THE FIFTH MYSTERY

The Fifth Mystery is connected with the fifth, or Seed Layer
of the earth, as it is designated in occult terminology. Into this
earth sheath is reflected the highest region of the mental world
which is known as the realm of Abstract Thought. It is at this
level or plane that mind is linked to spirit.

It is familiar knowledge that the origin of life is to be
found in seed. However it is not generally understood that
the origin of thought is also to be found in seed. In the Seed,
or fifth, earth Layer are stored the seed thoughts generated
by all mankind. If a person thinks intensely for a length of time
upon a specific idea, a seed thought of like nature will become
implanted in this realm. There it will germinate and bring forth
fruit of its kind. Such being the effects of the creative power of
mind, not only the person who brings such seed into being will
reap results therefrom, but others also will be influenced or

affected by it in varying degrees according to their affinity with what the seed produces. Thus, for example, when a powerful individual like an Alexander the Great or a Napoleon sets his mind on conquering the world, the results that spring from the seed generated therefrom can affect others of like mind for centuries to come through the original seed being multiplied many times over. Naturally the law operates in like manner for those possessed of high and noble thoughts. The good seed thought generated by St. Francis of Asissi, for example, has never ceased to bear fruit, and so, for example, it continues to be with that sown into our world by a modern saint like Mahatma Gandhi.

When a man is about to begin a new earth pilgrimage he is brought to this fifth earth layer there to begin the building of his new seed pattern. For as man lives today so is he building for tomorrow. It is in the Fifth Mystery that one is taught to read the record of past earth lives in the Memory of Nature, and to trace them through the seed patterns.

There is a line of demarcation which separates the first five of the nine Lesser Mysteries from the last four. Through the first five Mysteries the participant recapitulates and brings to perfection the work that is given to the early novitiate. This embraces purification and control of the desire nature and a spiritualizing of the mind which renders the mind receptive and obedient to the dictates of the spirit rather than subject to the inclinations and impulses of the personality.

As one passes through the first five of the lesser Mysteries the Christ within man is awakened and comes to govern his actions. As he passes into the exaltation of the four final and higher Degrees the Christ within comes into full flowering. Henceforth it is a God-man that participates in the sacred initiatory rites.

The Fifth is generally known as the Victory Symphony. This designation is most significant in its spiritual interpretation. It implies much more than the victory of man over man or nation over nation, for it refers to a conquest over self. The wisest of all biblical sages knew well the meaning of this conquest of self when he said, "Greater is he that controlleth himself than he that taketh a city."

The Fifth Mystery marks a transition period in the life of the aspirant. It is here that the last fetters of the personal life are broken so that the spirit may soar free and unfettered into Elysian heights. This transition period marks the merging of time with the timeless and the finite with the infinite. St. Paul described this momentous change as the putting off of the old man and the putting on of the new.

In his magnificent Fifth Symphony, Beethoven depicts this transition period in which the spell of the flesh is broken and the power of the spirit reigns supreme. One can never fully comprehend and appreciate the tremendous force and impact of the Fifth Symphony until he is qualified to interpret it spiritually. Then it is that one stands in spirit upon the shores of a vast uncharted sea, made luminous by the wonder of the mystery, yes, and with the terror as well as the beauty of the new and the unexplored, while above, myriads of celestial voices are heard chanting triumphantly. You now stand upon the threshold of Life Eternal which leads at last to a union with that most blessed One who is the Light of the World.

Chapter VI

BEETHOVEN'S SIXTH SYMPHONY IN F MAJOR

There's music in the sighing of a reed,
There's music in the gushing of a rill,
There's music in all things, if men had ears.
The earth is but an echo of the spheres.
— *Lord Byron*

The Sixth Symphony is one of the finest pieces in the whole range of absolute music. Beethoven never once transgressed the great principles of form and balance in this symphony. The opening movement is a true country picture full of the tonics and dominants of summer happiness. The scent by the brook with its drowsy reiterated figure on the undercurrent of divided strings is the very burden ever sounding in Nature herself. — *Romaine Rolland* in BEETHOVEN

Beethoven was a great poet who held nature by one hand and man by the other. — *Author Unidentified*

THE SIXTH SYMPHONY was completed in 1808 and was first presented in Vienna in the same year.

There is a cosmic triangle composed of God, Man and Nature. Man is the little god in the Grand Man. The more closely man comes into attunement with God the more deeply does he enter into the mysteries of nature.

It is quite significant that for the Sixth, or Nature Symphony, Beethoven chose the key of F major. Madame Blavatsky states in the *Secret Doctrine* that F is the musical keynote of earth and green is its color. Students of music therapy are well aware of the fact that the use of musical compositions in this key will produce beneficial effects upon various forms of nervous tension and upon pronounced and prolonged effects of insomnia. Anyone who has become tired and debilitated from overstrain and who has slipped away to spend even a single night in a pine forest breathing its soothing fragrance can never again doubt the healing ministration of nature nor the rejuvenating effects of the color green, for in very truth this is the color of life itself.

43

In his *Essaes de Technique et d'Esthetique Musicales*, M. W'lie Poiree observes that Beethoven's Pastoral Symphony which is done in F major has a "color-audition" corresponding to the color green. Understanding as he did the deep spiritual import of the different musical keys, Beethoven chose with the greatest care the keynote of each of his nine symphonies.

Also to be noted is the fact that the keynote of the Sixth Symphony is correlated to Virgo, the sixth sign of the zodiac. Virgo is a feminine sign and belongs to the earth triplicity. It is therefore attuned to Mother Nature. Its symbol is the Virgin bearing a sheaf of wheat. Among the spiritual keynotes of Virgo is Service by means of Tone and Beauty. These attributes also characterize the musical motifs of Beethoven's beautiful Sixth, or, as it is popularly designated, the Pastoral Symphony.

In this symphony, which is truly "a sublime Hymn to Nature," Beethoven sought to transcribe something of the harmonies existing in the operations of the cosmic triangle of God, Nature and Man. Hence it expresses much more than a journey through the woods or a ramble amid sylvan scenes. In the sudden summer storm so graphically conveyed in the fourth movement, Beethoven is describing the battle for supremacy between nature's elementals which always occurs in a tempest. The thunder is the voice of Air, the lightning of Fire and the rain of Water, the storm being their struggle for dominion over Earth. This is a magnificent sight and sound for those who have the eyes to see and the ears to hear. The hauntingly beautiful music of the Song in the Finale is a direct transcription for human bearing of the music of those Celestial Beings who guide and direct the life and activities throughout all nature. As Beethoven himself testified, "In the fields I seem to hear every tree repeating 'Holy, Holy, Holy.'"

Of the second movement, the Andante, designated by the composer as a "Scene by a Brook," Vincent d'Indy says "It is the most admirable expression of genuine nature in existence," adding that "there are only a few passages in Wagner's Siegfried and Parsifal that may be compared with it." Apropos the comparison here drawn, it may be recalled that Wagner in his work sought to combine in his music-dramas what Beethoven sought to express in his symphonies and Shakespeare in his dramas. It may well be, therefore, that the rare "nature" passages in Wagner took their inspiration from this very Pastoral Symphony of Beethoven.

To again quote Mr. D'Indy in his commentary on the second movement: "While the flow of the stream provides a foundation for the entire movement, lovely melodies expressively rise up out of it, and the feminine theme of the initial allegro reemerges alone, as though uneasy at its companion's absence. Each section in the movement is completed by the entrance of a theme of a few notes, pure as a prayer. It is the artist who speaks, who prays, who loves, and who takes delight in crowning the divisions of his work with a sort of Alleluia. This expressive theme terminates the expositions, twines about the steps of the development, in the midst of which the obscure tonalities cause a shadow to pass over the land. Then, following the somewhat light episodes of the bird-songs it is again thrice repeated, to conclude the whole with a touching affirmation."

The message of this symphony is as Beethoven phrased it, "An arrival at a knowledge of God through Nature."

As one writer has admirably defined Beethoven's faith which was cosmic rather than creedal, "Nature was Beethoven's Divinity; from her he had learned to accept all phenomena as reflections of the Godhead. He felt himself to be a chosen vessel of supernatural revelation, a hero, a saviour, who had suffered, and rising, had felt the divine life within him. . . . To the doctrine of Nature in God and God in Nature, of God imminent in the universe, he added a mystical apprehension of God as dwelling in one single artistic, creative individual."

There is a vast symphony forever playing throughout nature, a rare symphony of harmony and beauty that is inaudible to human ears and invisible to human eyes until one has raised consciousness to the point where it can commune with the powers functioning on the inner side of life. The sound of the wind in the trees, the rumble of the storm, the patter of the rain, the plaintive call of the cuckoo and the tender sound of the nightingale's song which are so graphically transcribed in this symphony, are but one aspect of nature's beauty and harmony. In exquisite and ethereal strains the composer transmits the rarified music of the up-springing of tender grass, the unfurling of flower petals, the swelling of new life forces in out-bursting leaves, in the rhythmic motion of airy sprites and the joyous singing of angelic beings — all these delicate and intangible things which belong to the hidden side of nature Beethoven has expressed in the second and third movements with such tremulous delicacy and airy beauty that their highest interpretations have probably not yet been fully rendered.

Beethoven was a profound musical philosopher who possessed not only the faculty of perceiving the life side of nature but also had the incomparable gift of transcribing something of the spiritual language for all to hear. All, however, have not developed the sensitivity to perceive the spiritual overtones which Beethoven was able to impart into his divinely inspired compositions. But they are there awaiting recognition as humanity rises in consciousness sufficiently to accompany the composer into the realms from which he drew his lofty inspiration. Meanwhile, those who are not yet able to partake fully in all that the composer experienced in the creation of his immortal works are nevertheless beneficiaries from what they do hear in a far more vital sense than is generally recognized. Music derives from the heaven world and whether man is aware of the fact or not, it serves to preserve in him, however faintly it may be, some recollection of the divine spheres from which he came and to which he is destined to return. It becomes a major factor in preventing man from falling into forgetfulness of his true home.

And so in hearing Beethoven's Pastoral Symphony, man's spirit is actually brought into a contact with more than impressions of external nature whatever may be the degree of his conscious perception of what is thus contacted. It is there; it impinges upon his finer vehicles, it leaves an impress that is refining, sensitizing, constructive, redemptive.

Hence it is not just nature music as this term is generally understood that Beethoven has given the world in his Pastoral. It is not an attempt to describe programmatically physical scenes and atmospheric effects. For those who can perceive the spiritual nuances of this symphonic creation, lilting bird songs convey angelic communications, flowing waters convey an inner peace, the open fields expanded horizons, while forests are transformed into vast cathedrals and mountains into lofty citadels of God.

THE SIXTH MYSTERY

The spiritual keynote of the Sixth Symphony is Unity. Six is a number that expresses light, love and beauty. These are the prevailing musical moods of the Sixth Symphony.

The Sixth Symphony is correlated with the sixth layer of the earth. This is the Fiery Stratum. In this connection we must not consider fire in the literal sense for this sixth layer of the earth is luminous with light. The occultist understands the difference between Fire and Flame. Fire is a spiritual force and Flame is the material aspect of that force. Moses stood before the flaming bush which was not consumed, which means that he stood in the presence of a spiritual being of Light that burned but did not consume.

This sixth earth layer reflects the spiritual forces of that high realm which is known metaphysically as the world of Christ Consciousness. It is the realm in which all sense of separateness has been transcended and the true universality of all life is realized. Here complete unity prevails. If, in obedience to St. John's admonition, we walk in the light as He is in the light, we will have fellowship one with another. Such is the effect of the music of the Sixth Symphony that one may well surmise that it was composed under the inspiration of the sublime vision of the all-inclusive, harmonious fellowship existing on this higher, spiritual plane of being.

Beethoven was ever nourishing in his heart the ideal of human brotherhood. It was deep and intense; it touched upon the unusual and the cosmic. In the Sixth is projected these qualities in relation to Nature, the externalization of God in whom man lives and moves and has his being. It is on this same ideal of brotherhood that he carries the listener on wings of ecstasy to heights of glory in the Finale in the last of his mighty Nine. It is only as this state of consciousness is developed that the inner glories of Nature can be revealed and that the sublime work of the Sixth Mystery can be successfully undertaken.

As stated previously, after the Fifth Initiation the work becomes so exalted that little can be said about it. To interpret something of this Sixth Mystery, Beethoven invoked the spirit of Nature. As man studies nature with ever increasing reverence and devotion, the more her sublime mysteries are revealed to him, and the closer becomes his attunement with God. A wise teacher has given to aspirants who seek to enter into life's deeper mysteries the admonition to "study nature, for it bears the imprint of divinity."

Beethoven heeded this admonition. This is how he expressed his faith in the wisdom to be learned, a passage that he copied so that he might have it ever with and before him. Thus: "One might rightly denominate Nature the school of the heart; she clearly shows us our duties toward God and our neighbor. Hence, I wish to become a disciple of this school and offer Him my heart. Desirous of instruction, I would seek after that wisdom which no disillusionment can confute; I would gain a knowledge of God and through this knowledge I shall obtain a foretaste of celestial felicity."

The Sixth Mystery is related to the Fire Initiation. The secret of life is connected with fire, and it is in the Sixth Mystery that one comes before this mighty truth. Here one learns to distinguish between *flame* and *fire*. Flame is recognizable by the five physical senses whereas the *spirit* of fire is perceived only through spiritual faculties. One who knows the secrets of the Fire Initiation can pass unharmed through flame. Various examples of this are recorded in that most profound of occult books, the Bible. Such are the translation of Elijah into heaven in a chariot of fire, the passing of the three holy men through fire as recorded in the Book of Daniel, and the tongues of flame that rested on the heads of the disciples at Pentecost. These are all descriptions of various stages or aspects of Initiation by Fire, and all relate in some degree to the Sixth Mystery.

The incarnational cycles through which the individualized spirit is destined to pass is the process by which the divine potentialities are awakened and developed into a living flame. This is the light to which St. John referred when he said, "If we walk in the light as He is in the light we shall have fellowship one with another." It is only as a man awakens this light within himself that he can ever know the true meaning of fellowship. Mankind can offer its Creator no greater gift than that of bringing into manifestation a universal fellowship and a united world.

Chapter VII

THE SEVENTH SYMPHONY IN A MAJOR

Beethoven composed the seventh of his Nine Symphonies "in all the exuberance of his creative maturity and each of its four movements brims over with the fiery essence of his inspiration. The listener is overpowered by the very lavishness of its beauty. In this symphony you feel Beethoven's genius as something inexhaustible, glorying in its own titanic power, as of a high god ignoring lesser breeds, proud of the knowledge of invincible strength, unfettered, care-free, save where the Alegretto acknowledges a divine melancholy. — *Pitts Sanborn*

THIS SYMPHONY was given its first performance in Vienna, December 8, 1813, thus making a five-year interval between the Sixth and the Seventh. During this period Beethoven was deepening his spiritual consciousness and coming into ever closer attunement with the forces of celestial music. What he produced in the Seventh offers ample evidence for the truth of Mr. Sanborn's evaluation as given above.

The spiritual keynote of the Seventh Symphony is Exaltation. Seven marks the completion of a cycle in terms of duration or time. The trine of spirit rises triumphant over the four-square of matter. The spiritual has now become primary, the material secondary. It is this triumph of Spirit which is the glorious theme-song of the Seventh. Both Richard Wagner and Franz Liszt regarded the symphony as the "apotheosis of the dance." The innermost spirit of the dance enacts rhythmically the ascent on the initiatory path which concludes in divine at-one-ment with Light Eternal. From this standpoint of interpretation the Seventh Symphony is truly an Apotheosis of the Dance.

Wagner identified this Symphony with the dance in its highest expression as the realization of the body in ideal form. None knew better than he that the dance had its origin in the movements of the planetary spheres and that the mission of Beethoven was to recapture something of these stellar harmonies.

In the first movement (Pocco sostenuto, vivace), dominant, exultant chords iterate and reiterate this triumphant song to the accompaniment of the intoxicating rhythm of the main theme. This introduction unfolds the themes that follow in a succession of ascending scales that have been described as gigantic stairs. Beethoven is here attuning human ears to planetary rhythms. He brings to earth intimations of the music of the spheres by which solar systems are propelled in their courses. Thus his music really does become a stairway that mounts to the stars. He carries the hearer to great heights and depths, transcending the little, cramped sphere in which mortal man moves in his uninspired state.

In the second movement (Allegretto) a note of solemnity is introduced. It passes from A Major into A Minor, since it is easier to recapture the echoings of celestial music in minors. It is as if the spirit were awed at the realization of the responsibility that comes with such high attainment. This solemn, mysterious note persists throughout the entire movement. It has been likened to a procession through the catacombs.

The third movement (Presto, presto meno assai) strikes a yet more exultant note than was heard in the first. Gay, exciting rhythms are introduced by the strings with a joyous response from the woodwinds. There are dancing arpeggios and a scherzo spirit throughout.

The Finale (Allegro con brio) is colossal and magnificent. It is as if heaven and earth joined in a mighty chorusing of majesty and power. It is the voice of the spirit ecstatically proclaiming: "I am free, I am free, for all time and eternity. I am free."

This exultant spirit of freedom has quite naturally called into expression the companion art of the dance. Wagner, previously quoted in this connection, felt that there was nothing so dull or dead that could withstand its magic spell, the benches, cans and cups, the blind and the lame, and so on, would fall to dancing.

The celebrated Isadora Duncan danced all but the first movement of this symphony at the Metropolitan Opera House in New York in 1908, and the Ballet Russe of Monte Carlo also transcribed the entire work into the poetry of motion. That the choreography the symphony evokes has more of an ethereal and spiritual character than physical, is voiced by one commentator who thought of it as expressing a ceremonial dance such as might have been performed by the Corybants, the priests of Cybele, round the cradle of the infant Zeus.

A VISION OF THE PATH

In musical retrospect, as it were, a traveller approaches a vast towering mountain, the snow-crowned summit of which glistens in the sunlight like a multi-diamond crown. The ascent of this mountain is steep and perilous, the path narrow and precipitous. Ofttimes the traveller loses his footing, and lies prone upon the ground, but always the quiet inner Voice firmly urges, "Onward and upward forever." Sometimes he takes the wrong turn and must retrace his steps over the long and narrow way, but always the inner Voice, gentle but insistent, is heard to say, "you will never fail so long as you persist, for the only failure is in ceasing to try." Again the path leads through dark and narrow crevasses where the sun is lost to view. It is then that only in his mind's eye can he see the snowy height above. The summit is surrounded by great masses of perpendicular rocks concealing all view of the path. To accomplish the ascent the traveller must possess dauntless courage, steadfast persistence and a will that is dominated by spirit.

At last the summit attained and oh! the wondrous glory of the view! Far below are plains and valleys surrounded by low-lying hills interspersed by sparkling streams. There are also great cities in which mankind plies its daily routine, the majority being too busy or too careless to lift their eyes and catch the inspiration of the beautiful white peaks towering above.

As the traveller lifts his eyes upward he is filled with amazement, for the summit on which he stands, which he thought so high and so final, is dwarfed by yet loftier peaks beyond, whose crests are completely lost to view in the vast blue. The words of the mystic poet, Kahlil Gibran, come to mind with a new-born significance: "When you have reached the mountain top, then you shall begin to climb."

It is then that the traveller cries out "What is beyond the majestic peaks whose heights are lost in the skies?" And the Voice, in joyous exaltation replies, "Infinity." "And what is beyond Infinity?" Like a benediction from far away places, in tones of unearthly sweetness the Voice replies, "An Infinity of Infinities."

This is the soul-song of Beethoven's Seventh Symphony, the spirit triumphant and exultant, singing "Ever onward and upward forever and ever, for the Path of Truth is endless and the Quest is Eternal."

THE SEVENTH MYSTERY

The Seventh Mystery is connected with the seventh earth stratum known as the Reflecting Layer. This stratum correlates with the World of Divine Spirit and is permeated with the spiritual power of this high heavenly realm.

True to its descriptive name, the reflecting stratum in the earth reacts accurately to the nature of man's thoughts and desires. These are both constructive and destructive, for under karmic law of cause and effect both men and nations react as they sow. Such is the Divine Law as it operates in the world of Divine Spirit, which is the higher counterpart of the earth's reflecting stratum.

Thus, for example, on the destructive side occult history records the submerging of the continent Atlantis and destruction of its advanced civilization due to the widespread practice of black magic. In historical times we read of the fall of Babylon, one of the earth's most beautiful and famous cities, its hanging gardens having been classed among the Seven Wonders of the World. In Pompeii archaeologists have uncovered evidences of the moral laxity and depravity which existed among the inhabitants which reacted through the forces located in the fiery stratum of the earth in the natural disaster that buried the city in flowing lava and ashes. Also, in the Bible, we read of the destruction of Sodom and Gomorrah due to the evils rampant in these two cities.

Man is a sevenfold being. The threefold spirit is connected with the threefold body by the link of mind. The chief purpose

of man's many earthly pilgrimages is to enable the threefold
spirit to work upon the threefold body in order to refine,
sensitize and spiritualize these lower bodies and transmute
them into soul powers.

Before one is ready to pass through the portal leading into
the Seventh Mystery, much of this work must necessarily have
been accomplished. In the seventh or reflecting earth layer is
to be found what are termed the seven great secrets of nature.
These secrets are connected with the four elements, Fire, Air,
Water and Earth. In this degree one learns many varying ways
in which these elements are transmuted with results enabling
one to control many of Nature's Laws. The Seventh is the
Degree of Divine Sublimation. When one has passed through
this Degree the power attained makes possible the journeying
into the lowest depths of the earth and into the heights of
outer space.

The Initiate of the Seventh Mystery is taught to investigate
and understand more deeply something of the fourfold powers
known as Fire, Air Water and Earth. These powers operate
under the direction of high celestial beings. Very little can
be said openly regarding this work except that under the
power of Fire and Air new and greater secrets are taught which
are concerned with transmutation and under those of Water
and Earth are taught the most profound meanings concerning
equilibrium or polarity.

In that exalted sphere where the Initiate is brought face
to face with the truths belonging to the Seventh Mystery he
becomes a veritable miracle worker. He learns what it means
to pass unharmed through fire and water, to overcome the law
of gravitation and to work in harmony with the law of levitation.
He is now a true white magician having learned to turn, as
it were, base metals into gold. He has gained freedom from the
bondage and limitation which this planet imposes upon him. It is
something of this wonderful Spirit of Freedom which is described
in the glorious unforgettable music of the Seventh Symphony.

Such is the magic wielded by the music of Beethoven's
Seventh that Philip Hale, commentator, truly observed, "Whenever the music is played, whenever it comes into the mind, it

awakens new thoughts and each one dreams his own dreams."

There is such a mystical power infused into this symphony that it has the magic of awakening in the soul of an aspirant a vision of the steps that lead progressively up the ladder of attainment. More than that, it actually radiates tonal energies that impart a strength to the soul on the initiatory path to take those steps until the quest is finally consummated in the supernal glories of the realm Elysian.

Chapter VIII

THE EIGHTH SYMPHONY IN F MAJOR

Never has an art offered the world anything so serene as the symphonies in A and F major and all those works so intimately related to them which the master produced during the divine period of his deafness. Their first effect upon a hearer is that of setting him free from a sense of guilt, while their after-effect gives rise to a feeling of paradise being lost as he turns again toward the world of phenomena. Thus these wonderful works preach repentance and atonement in the sense of divine revelation.

In this symphony there are exquisite musical thoughts; there are passages that for a moment sound the depths and reach the heights. . . . Without the grandeur of the Fifth or the romance of the Seventh, it contains a lasting if less easy charm, perfect finish, and a rich fund of good humor. — *Romaine Rolland*

THE EIGHTH SYMPHONY had its first performance in Vienna April 20, 1813. Its spiritual keynote is Harmony.

The ancients declared that the number eight bears the impress of divinity, and this gives the signature of the Eighth Symphony. Berlioz declares that the pattern of this Symphony was formulated in heaven and dropped into the brain of its composer. An art critic writing of this Symphony says that it is a divine play in the region of tonal thinking. Further, that as the Seventh Symphony is epic art at its best, so the Eighth Symphony is lyric art at its highest. The Eighth has also been called "an epic of humor." Its four divisions are permeated with a breath of joyousness and abounds in whimsical humor. A light and fanciful spirit of happiness pervades it throughout. It is altogether delightful in its entirety. Beethoven was said to have regarded it with tenderness and referred to it as his "little one." Perhaps this was because of its lighthearted spirit, and also because it is the shortest of the Nine.

The first two parts abound with the spirit of joy and their entrancing harmonies continue to weave and interweave throughout the third part. Instead of the usual Scherzo this third movement is a beautiful and stately minuet. While delicately fanciful, it at the same time touches a deeper note. It has been likened by some writers to exultant laughter. This is indeed true. It does sound the triumphant laughter of the emancipated soul who has found his own divine heritage of conscious immortality and the divine bliss of cosmic freedom. As Pitts Sanborn writes it is "not the laughter of childish glee or of a reckless, despairing levity." Rather, it is the "vast and inextinguishable laughter" Shelly speaks of in *Prometheus Unbound.* It is the laughter of a man who has loved and suffered, and scaling the heights, achieved the summit. Only here and there does a note of rebellion momentarily obtrude itself; and here and there in lyrical repose . . . an intimation of Divinity more than the ear discovers."

The Finale ascends into illimitable heights in both tempo and fantasy. Sudden irregularities and interrupted rhythms serve to create an atmosphere of deliberate mystification. It is highly charged fantasy designed to carry the hearer beyond the narrow confines of the concrete mind.

The Eighth Symphony is yet another composition that Beethoven's great creative genius has given to man to assist him in laying hold of the spiritual purposes which it was his true destiny to pursue and to fulfill.

Erwin Grove in his work *Beethoven's Nine Immortals,* describes Beethoven's power to abstract himself from the outer world and live in a dream world of his own. His ideal, like those of all great heroes, had little interest in the world and the small people around him. He was a lofty, lonely mountain peak looking across the valleys towards his mighty peers. His eyes bore witness to a lonely spiritually hungry man. His idealism overrode his judgment. It was difficult for him to accept things as they really were rather than as he idealized them. In his later years he melted into profound tenderness and sweet wistfulness, resulting in what was termed his "feminine tendency." He learned, as did Samson, through suffering and sorrow that "out of the eater came forth meat and out of the strong came forth sweetness."

Beethoven was an instrument used by the Spirit of Music

to realize itself rather than a man who merely wrote music. In his music, always creating new worlds, his greatest genius was shown in his fast movements for they reflect rhythms of heavenly orbs which move with greater speed than light.

Gustav Nottebohn, in his *Sketches of Eroica* observes that Beethoven achieved a type of melody some called *absolute* and in composing his supreme works he was veritably "possessed." His Higher Mind took over. He then worked not from the particular to the whole but began with the whole and worked back to particulars. Under a kind of subconscious state of mind a composition possessed him as a whole before he began to think out the details. A poet expressed this same truth in the words, "You would not have sought me unless you had already found me."

We have referred repeatedly to the Nine Symphonies as *cosmic* music. As Beethoven wrote them, they were obviously to demonstrate musically the fundamental truths of Polarity. The odd-numbered symphonies possess the grandeur, flight, daring, courage, innovation or all the dominant masculine qualities. The even-numbered ones are sweet, gentle, tender, docile, calm, characteristic of the feminine.

The Fifth in C Minor would have followed the Third, or the *Eroica* had Beethoven carried out the sketches as they originally came to him, according to his biographers. Something in his nature forestalled this until the gentler symphony in B Major, the Fourth, had inserted itself into a divine pattern which placed it immediately after the mighty royal expenditure of the Third.

Then following the Epic Fifth, there follows the Sixth or Pastoral Symphony as a contemplative companion.

Again, after a space of four years Beethoven produced another pair of complementary affinities: the Seventh, of masculine strength and the Eighth of feminine attributes, the two produced in 1862 in close succession.

Finally, almost ten years later there came forth the magnificent blending of the opposites, as these had alternated in ascendancy in the preceding eight symphonies in the supreme, culminating grandeur of the Ninth.

THE EIGHTH MYSTERY

The Eighth Mystery is connected with the eighth earth sheath known as the Atomistic Layer. The power of this mystery is such that an object posited in this layer when used as a nucleus may be multiplied at will. It was the power of this Eighth Mystery that the Master was demonstrating to the disciples when He multiplied the five loaves and the two fishes and fed five thousand — with twelve full baskets remaining.

Very little can be said about this Mystery excepting that the participant must have gained mastery over both himself and the outer objective world. A basic harmony is a requisite for entrance into this exalted Rite. The essences of experience gained through all the preceding mysteries are here builded into soul power of such strength that an all-abiding harmony becomes the keynote of life. No longer will such a one experience emotional outbursts, nor be unduly swayed by events either painful or pleasurable. He has now found for all time that profound inner calm and peace to which St. Paul referred when he said in effect none of the things of the outer world moved him.

The celestial sphere termed occultly the World of Virgin Spirits is reflected in the eighth layer of the earth. It is at this level of being that God differentiates within Himself the entities that constitute an evolutionary life wave. It is from this plane that these divine beings in embryo enter upon their long aeonic evolutionary journey through time and space and matter. At this stage the Virgin Spirits possess only divine consciousness. The ends to be attained through their involution into matter is self-consciousness from which stage the evolutionary process is to carry them back to God-consciousness with self-consciousness having been added thereto.

In the Eighth Mystery the Initiate is lifted far beyond the world of man. Words are altogether inadequate to describe the wonders and the glories of that spiritual realm into which he is permitted to enter. The sublime music of the Eighth Symphony transcribes some of the wonders of this realm.

Every illumined soul sings his own Song of Achievement. This song is sometimes an utterance of aspiration, questing, travail, disillusionment and even of utter darkness. Then as the quest continues, there follows new and fresh and ever deepening dedication which culminates eventually into a victory of complete self-conquest. This was the soul-song Moses sang at the victory of the Red Sea, a victory which referred not so much to a physical occurrence as to a perfected transmutation within himself. Other soul songs of such attainment are David's immortal twenty-third Psalm and St. Paul's greatest of all love songs, the thirteenth chapter of I Corinthians. Such also is the Swan Song of Lohengrin in that superb music-drama which bears his name. It is this same Song of Achievement which is heard in Beethoven's Eighth Symphony, composed not in words but in the language of tone drawn inspirationally from the heavenly world of tone. The Finale of this Symphony resounds with all the deep joy of an Emancipated One. It is the Soul Song of one who has by his inherent divinity learned to claim his divine heritage which is Cosmic Freedom. This is the keynote of the Eighth Mystery and is the exalted musical theme of the Eighth Symphony.

The exalted work of this eighth Mystery is exemplified in the music of the Eighth Symphony which is so soft, beautiful and filled with such an undercurrent of strength that seems to sing of the ability to calm the raging tempest or to remove mountains from their places. The music of the Eighth Symphony is expressive of the high perfected Feminine, that supreme spiritual power which the alchemist described as the Feminine in Exaltation.

Chapter IX

THE NINTH SYMPHONY IN D MINOR

(With Final Chorus on Schiller's *Ode to Joy*)

Music is the one incorporeal entrance into the higher world of knowledge which comprehends mankind but which mankind cannot comprehend. —
For sheer beauty of idea there is little in the realm of music that can approach this masterpiece in beautiful melody. Its ideas are so rich in their variety, so delicate in their orchestration, and withal so profoundly sympathetic, that he must be a hardened listener indeed who can hearken to this movement without some perception of a vision of the heavens opening, and of a distant gaze into some world beyond this. Here we have Beethoven as an exponent of the sublime. . . . No one will deny that here is a masterpiece unequalled in the tremendous vastness of its conception, and unapproachable for its originality, power, and lavishly scattered beauties. — *Author unidentified.*

MORE THAN TEN YEARS passed after the initial performance of the Eighth Symphony before Beethoven brought out its successor, his Ninth and last, on May 7th, 1824. During this interval there was evidently a deep preparation going on within himself that was to eventuate ultimately with the glorious climactic creation, the Ninth Symphony.

When the Lords of Destiny seek to choose a messenger whose mission will benefit the world and uplift mankind, much time and care are given to the choice. Special precautions are taken that such a chosen one will not fall a prey to the seductions of the material world. Beethoven was such a chosen messenger. He was born in poverty and reared under the most adverse circumstances. All the years of his life were filled with loneliness, disappointment and disillusionment with the things of the outer world.

A messenger thus chosen for a high world mission seldom knows the joys of human companionship which is the privilege of most mortals. He must necessarily live a more or less detached life. Much time must be spent alone in order that he may reach

those inspirational heights which will enable him to become a
clear and unobstructed channel for his appointed work.

At the time of Beethoven's funeral it was said, "He had no
wife to weep for him — no son, no daughter — but all the world
mourns at his bier." The life of such a one is centered not in
the one but in the many. Hence when Beethoven reached the
prime of life there came to him, according to human understanding, the greatest misfortune that can ever befall a musician,
the loss of his hearing. However, from a spiritual viewpoint
this was perhaps his greatest blessing. He was to be a messenger
to bring through the glorious celestial music of the Creative
Hierarchies. This music is so sublime and ethereal that the dis-
cordant and inharmonious earth tones were not to obstruct and
impair its purity and beauty. And so when Beethoven lost his
physical hearing he became increasingly sensitive to inner plane
harmonies and hence a more perfect transmitter for this heavenly
music. Even though the spirit may be aware of its high destiny,
so long as it is confined within the human body it will have to
contend with the limitations of its mortal instrument. And so it
was that at times Beethoven gave way to melancholy and despair,
sometimes shaking his fist in the face of Fate.

The true purpose of sorrow is to serve as a purifying and
redeeming agent. In *Light on the Path*, which is one of the most
illumined spiritual manuals ever written, it is stated that "before
the eyes can see they must have lost their sense of separative-
ness, and that before the ears can hear they must have lost their
sensitiveness, and before the feet can stand in the presence of
the Masters they must be washed in the blood of the heart."

As Edward Carpenter writes about Beethoven in his *Angels'
Wings*, "Though his outer life, by deafness, disease, business
worries, poverty was shattered as it were into a thousand
squalid fragments — in his great heart he embraced all mankind,
with piercing insight penetrated intellectually through all false-
hoods to the truth, and already in his art-work gave outline to
the religious, the human, the democratic yearnings, the loves,
the comradeship, the daring individualities and all the heights
and depths of feeling of a new era of society. He was in fact,
and he gave utterance to, a new type of man. What that struggle

must have been between his inner and outer conditions — of his real self with the lonely and mean surroundings in which it was embodied—we only know through his music. When we listen to it we can understand the world-old tradition that now and then a divine creature from far heavens takes mortal form and suffers in order that it may embrace and redeem mankind."

The spiritual keynote of the Ninth Syhphony is Consummation. Nine is the most important number in relation to mankind's present stage in evolution. It is the number of humanity. It is also the number of Initiation, that straight and narrow path by which man returns to a union with God.

It has been noted previously that Beethoven's symphonies portray a variety of experiences. These experiences are recapitulated in the ever ascending steps up the spiritual path of attainment, each repetition giving added strength and glory of soul unfoldment until the consummation is attained in the divine oneness so magnificently interpreted in the Ninth.

As previously indicated, the symphonies carrying odd numbers embody the masculine attributes and the even numbers the feminine, while in the last or Ninth the two attributes are brought into perfect equilibrium, a state of unity which in esoteric parlance is termed the Mystic Marriage. This union marks man's supreme earthly attainment. Hence it is, that the music descriptive of this development is not by chance the highest and most glorious that has ever been brought to earth. Beethoven caught that beautiful chorusing of the Cherubim in the glory of the Ninth, so that human ears could catch the mighty outpouring of its spiritual power.

One writer, John Maglee Burk, in his *Life and Works of Beethoven* refers to these heavenly echoings as "mysterious murmurings;" then, as if the whisperings from the inner world which Beethoven inwardly perceived, grew ever clearer and louder as the initial theme develops, there is "a crescendo of suspense until the theme itself is revealed . . . and proclaimed fortissimo by the whole orchestra in unison. No one," he adds, "has quite equalled the mighty effect of Beethoven's own precedent — not even Wagner, who held this particular page in mystic awe, and no doubt remembered it when he depicted the elementary serenity of the Rhine in a very similar manner at the opening of the *Ring*."

"That Ninth Symphony," writes Ralph Hill in his work entitled *The Symphony*, "is even by comparison with such mighty works as the *Eroica* and Fifth Symphonies, on a tonally different psychological plane, that it raises vaster issues than anything in Beethoven's previous symphonic writing, has been generally agreed. Each of its movements is unparalleled in constructive power and in the span and magnitude of its musical ideas. The opening is one of sustained mystery and intensity. From a region in which all seems nebulous and ill-defined . . . emerge the first faint foreshadowing of a theme which is presently hurtled at us with the force of Jove's thunderbolts. . . . This portentous opening is next restated . . . and the full subject transferred, still fortissimo, to the key of B flat. For the moment it is with the termination of this gigantic theme that we have to do, and this in rising sequences marches remorselessly onwards till we reach the transition to the second subject-group, which has been supposed to bear some faint resemblance to the *Joy* theme of the Finale."

"There can be scarcely anything finer in all music," writes E. Markham Lee in *The Story of Symphony*, "than the opening movement, so serenely simple, and at the same time so majestic in its ideas. Technically, its manifold manipulation of material is little short of marvellous, and its expressive qualities . . . are very great."

The second movement, a Scherzo, though not actually labelled as such, has been considered by many musical critics as one of Beethoven's most notable achievements. One writer has referrd to its "trippy gait" as "strongly intermixed with a mystic vein, a little like a dance of will-o'-the-wisps." Berlioz has compared it to the clear pure air that accompanies the sunrise on a bright May morning.

"Words fail us," writes Markham Lee, "to comment adequately upon the Adagio (third movement), one of the most perfectly beautiful pieces of orchestral music that can ever be penned." Bernard Shore, speaking of this third movement in his work *Sixteen Symphonies*, avers that it is music that "might be in the heavens," and notes how the incomparable Toscanini in rendering this part "made every effort to transfer the playing from brilliant, incisive vitality to the quietest, subdued tenderness. "In Paradiso,' he exclaimed. The strings particularly caressed their music and were never allowed to become passionate — only ethereal.

"The colossal first three movements of the Ninth Symphony are on the highest plane of all music. The opening theme of the first movement is mighty in inspiration, rugged in power. The Scherzo is perhaps Beethoven's very finest. The Adagio opens with a melody of the utmost nobility — perfect in curve and of a marvellous serenity. The devout feeling of mysticism and awe increases until the final chorus."

A MUSICAL HARBINGER OF THE NEW AGE

Beethoven experienced such an inner freedom of spirit, such an ecstatic state of soul. Consequently he was able to transcribe for human hearing the most sublime music this world has ever known. Sigmund Spaeth in his book *A Guide to Great Orchestral Music,* has phrased it perfectly: "The symphony reached in Beethoven its apogee. During the century that came after him great musicians composed much beautiful music in the form, but we have only to contemplate Beethoven to realize that the zenith was passed, and all music since is music in a long drawn afternoon."

Ludwig von Beethoven was one of the most important evangels of the New Age that ever came to earth. Each and every one of his magnificent musical compositions sounds the note of freedom, emancipation, equality and the eventual and permanent conquest of good over evil.

Beethoven also showed his complete harmony with New Age impulses in his ideal of womanhood and in the profound respect and reverence which he bestowed upon all womankind. He could never understand how Mozart could use his great genius depicting so many shallow and frivolous women. Beethoven gave to the world only one opera, *Fidelio,* the faithful one. In its heroine, Leonora, he gives a perfect picture of the New Age woman. The last of the three overtures to Leonora which is heard in the final act of the opera is a rhapsody descriptive of the exaltation of the Divine Feminine which must be awakened in all humanity before the glorious truths belonging to the New Age can become realities upon earth. The opera, *Fidelio*, concludes with a triumphant Choral depicting the glad day when freedom and brotherhood will have become universal throughout the world. It is these same keynotes of Freedom, Brotherhood and Universality that are heard in the choral with which he concludes his final and supreme work, the Ninth Symphony.

THE CHORAL TO THE NINTH SYMPHONY

The singer is translating his song into singing, his joy into forms, and the hearer has to translate back the singing into the original joy; then the communion between the singer and the hearer is complete. The infinite joy is manifesting itself in manifold forms, taking upon itself the bondage of law, and we fulfill our destiny when we go back from form to joy, from law to love, when we untie the knot of the finite and hark back to the Infinite. — *Rabindranath Tagore*

As previously mentioned, Beethoven was a selected messenger to transcribe cosmic music for human hearing. This "inner pressure led him to choose a life of self-abnegation and rectitude. He saw through and over and beyond the illusions and allurements of the world, in an age, and among a people, largely given over to the pursuit of pleasure."

By cosmic music we mean the music of the celestial Hierarchies. It was the triumphant music sounded forth by the Cherubim and Seraphim in celebration of the Mystic Marriage Rites of the Ninth Mystery which Beethoven has recorded in the magnificent Choral of the Ninth Symphony.

Mankind can never experience the high spiritual exaltation of this Rite until he has learned to build and live in a United World — a world in which the Fatherhood of God and the Brotherhood of Man shall have become the ideal realized. To further the ideal of universal brotherhood was his supreme aim; to this end his great genius was completely dedicated.

For the Choral Beethoven used Schiller's poem *The Ode to*

Joy. This poem which was written during the French Revolution, bears for its theme *Universal Brotherhood.*

> Praise to Joy, the God-descended
>   Daughter of Elisium!
> Ray of mirth and rapture blended
>   Goddess, to thy shrine we come!
> By thy magic is united
>   What stern custom parted wide,
> All mankind are brothers plighted
>   Where thy gentle wings abide.
> O ye millions, I embrace ye,
>   With a kiss for all the world!
> Brothers, o'er yon starry sphere
>   Surely dwells a loving Father.
> O ye millions, kneel before Him
>   World, dost feel thy Maker near?
>   Seek Him o'er yon starry sphere,
> O'er the stars enthroned, adore Him!
> Joy, thou daughter of Elysium,
>   By thy magic is united
> What stern custom parted wide.
>   All mankind are brothers plighted
> Where thy gentle wings abide.

For certain political reasons, Schiller does not use the word "Freedom," and so substituted for it the word *joy.* Beethoven understood this. For him the poem was an expression of spiritual freedom. It meant the emancipation of the soul; the freedom of the spirit from all physical and material limitations. It meant freedom to roam at will through the higher spiritual realms, to contact celestial beings who inhabit those realms and to listen to the glorious music of the spheres. In the first movement the heavens send forth mighty paens of evocation through the profound mysticism of D Minor which is proclaimed by the entire orchestra in unison.

Later the theme is repeated and the orchestra sounds the same note of triumph in D Major which tells us musically that the proclamations of the heavenly chorus have now descended to the earth realm.

The second movement Berlioz describes in all its inherent beauty as similar to the "effect of fresh morning air and the first rays of the rising sun in May."

The Adagio theme expresses itself in variations of increasingly

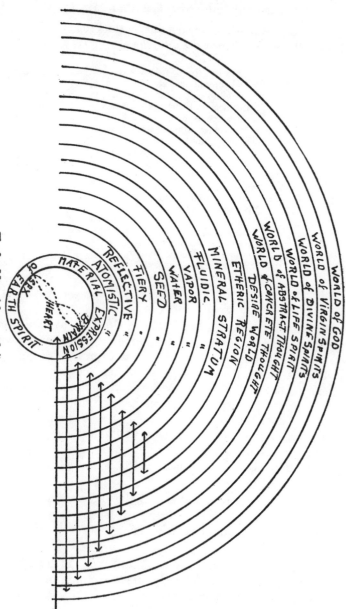

The Ladder of Spiritual Ascent

World of GOD
World of VIRGIN SPIRITS
World of DIVINE SPIRITS
World of LIFE SPIRIT
World of ABSTRACT THOUGHT
World of CONCRETE THOUGHT
DESIRE WORLD
ETHERIC REGION
MINERAL STRATUM
FLUIDIC. "
VAPOR "
WATER "
SEED "
FIERY "
REFLECTIVE "
ATOMISTIC "
MATERIAL EXPRESSION "
AXIS of EARTH SPIRIT
HEART
BRAIN

intricate and melodic ornamentation of that rare and indescribable beauty which characterizes Beethoven at his highest.

Each movement of his symphonies is a divine adventure in spirit. The spirit when awakened (illumined) can never be satisfied completely with only the gifts this physical realm has to offer.

The Finale speaks to us of this. It is questing, searching eagerly for even yet greater light. A hint of that high realization voiced by the choral theme is echoed softly by the woodwinds. The theme is then gradually unfolded in D Major (still an earth plane experience).

In the fourth movement Beethoven for the first time introduces words into a symphony. Schiller's *Ode to Joy* is the foundation of the Finale sung by solo, quartet and the chorus. Beethoven used this Ode to express human solidarity. This sublime chorus lifts earth closer to heaven and draws celestials into more intimate communion with mortals. It sounds the highest keynote of human achievement which is self-emancipation.

THE NINTH MYSTERY

The Ninth Mystery leads to the very heart of the earth. At this center is reflected the highest of all spiritual realms, the World of God. This is the realm where Absolute Good resides. Here spirit unites with matter, the finite merges with the Infinite, and God and man meet face to face.

It is here that the Gods of other planetary systems commune with the God of this system. It is here that the holy Mysteries of Creation are revealed. No music that has ever been given to this earth planet can translate the wonder and the glory of this sublime experience excepting the magnificent Choral with which the master Beethoven concludes the Ninth Symphony.

On Page 68 is inserted a diagram which outlines this ladder of celestial ascent. Few there are as yet upon the earth who have attained to its higher rungs.

Only those who have exchanged the personal for the impersonal, the terrestrial for the celestial, the human, for the divine and who have become truly Christed individuals achieve the highest spheres of consciousness. But to so attain is the high and glorious destiny awaiting all mankind as it makes itself worthy of the divine ascent.

On the Holy Night when the Ninth Mystery is celebrated, innumerable angelic Hosts fill the air with their ecstasy of song. The echoes of this glorious music of the heavens were captured by Beethoven and given to the world in the sublime Choral of his great Ninth Symphony.

Within the heart of the earth there are three power centers which correlate with the three principal centers in the human body-temple, namely, the head, the heart and the reproductive organs. Between the head and the reproductive centers there is an intimate relationship. Between these two focal points of creative energies there is a constant flow of the sacred life force. This takes the form of the lemniscate, the point of conjunction being in the heart. A like pattern of the divine creative energies are in action within the heart of the earth.

Participation in the Ninth Mystery is possible only after the currents above described have attained a state of perfect balance, with the mind spiritually illumined, the heart a transmitter of the still small voice within and the reproductive center a seat of the regenerated life force. This attainment is climaxed by coming face to face with the supreme Lord of this world, the Blessed Christ. Such is the glorious experience awaiting the soul that reaches the ninth step on the ladder of being, the Ninth Mystery.

The only music which can adequately describe the soul rapture of this experience is the magic which Beethoven has succeeded in weaving into his Ninth Symphony. It is only by means of such celestial music that something of its high spiritual import may be intoned. It is music such as can come only from the deepest spiritual experience of which man is capable of registering in his present limited being. It is the master magician's priceless gift to humanity to aid it in its conscious and unconscious reaching upward to recapture something more of its pristine divine estate.

With the writing of the Ninth Symphony Beethoven's work was completed, his destiny fulfilled. This was his swan song, his most magnificent accomplishment. This incomparable composition, as previously stated, was given to the world in 1824. Three years later, in 1827, he received the summons to come up higher. Then, no doubt, he, too, was found worthy to stand in the divine presence and to hear the benign words which have sounded down the ages, "Well done, thou good and faithful servant, enter thou into the joy of thy Lord."

EPILOGUE

THE NINE SYMPHONIES AND THE NINE MYSTERIES

As we look at pure instrumental music, we notice that in the symphony of Beethoven the greatest disorder reigns, and yet beneath all is the most absolute order: the most violent strife, which immediately becomes the sweetest concord. It is *rerum concordia discors*, a true and complete picture of the essential nature of the world, which rolls on in measureless complexity and numberless shapes, and supports itself by constant destruction. At the same time all human emotions and passions speak from this symphony, love and hate, fear and hope, all in the abstract only, and without any particularity; it is really the *form* of emotion, a spirit-world without matter. It is true, however, that we are inclined to *realize* it while listening, to clothe it in our fancy with flesh and blood, and to behold in it the various scenes of life and nature. — *Arthur Schopenhauer*

The Nine Mysteries which are described in this volume are observed at certain special times. These Observances take place in the Mystery Temples of the Great Brotherhoods which are located in the etheric sphere.

The First Mystery takes place at midnight on Saturday. A part of this sublime work is a recapitulation of that time in earth history known to occultists as the Saturn Period and is biblically described as the First Creative Day.

The Second Mystery is observed on Sunday at midnight. This, in addition to other work which has been previously mentioned, recapitulates the Sun Period of the earth's evolution which is biblically the Second Great Creative Day.

The Third Mystery is observed at midnight on Monday and recapitulates the work of the Moon Period, or Third Great Creative Day.

The Fourth Mystery is observed not only on one day but two. The first is at midnight on Tuesday and the second at midnight on Wednesday. This double observance is because the present Earth Period is divided into two distinct halves. The first half comes under the direction of Mars, under whose martial nature the earth's skies have been darkened with wars and rumors of war. The second observance on midnight of Wednesday reveals something of the wonders of the second, or Mercury half of the Earth Period. Mankind will then have attained to its ardently longed for dream of a peaceful and united world.

The Fifth Mystery is observed at midnight on Thursday when the glories of the next Period of Earth's evolution, the Jupiter Period will have come into being.

The Sixth Mystery is observed at midnight on Friday and contains the glorious revelations belonging to a still higher stage of this planet's development which bears the designation of the Venus Period.

The Seventh Mystery is observed at specifically fixed times on each night of the week, and is concerned with the work of this planet's last evolutionary Day which is known as the Vulcan Period.

The sublime Eighth Mystery is observed each month on the nights of the New and Full Moon.

The glory of the Ninth Mystery is consummated at the two highest spiritual points of the entire year, namely, midnight of the Winter and the Summer Solstices.

Beethoven spoke of a tenth symphony which was doubtless to describe musically this more exalted work. Although he left a number of notes for such a composition it was never completed. This evidently was not within the scope of his specific divine assignment. When mankind will be able to grasp something of its glorious destiny, as related to the first of the Greater Christ Mysteries, and only then, will a still higher musical interpreter be sent by the Hierarchy to convey musically, something of the transcendent powers, belonging to the Greater Christ Mysteries.

When one passes through the fourth of the nine Lesser Mysteries, he is hailed with great rejoicing by his brother Initiates and is known as "the newborn."

The work of the fifth of the Lesser Mysteries is concerned with the amalgamation of the essences of Fire, Air, Water and

Earth. This work is concerned not only with the operation of these elements throughout nature but also in relation to man himself. Fire correlates with man's desire nature, Air with the mind, Water with the emotional nature and Earth with the physical body. As the aspirant learns to control these forces within himself, he also gains control of their operation throughout nature. This gives him the ability to walk upon the water, to pass unharmed through fire, to journey at will through the air and to pass at will unobstructed through the inner planes of the earth. These things are known as the miracles of the Initiate.

As so few possess the ability at the present time to perform these so-called miracles, they are generally considered superstition and fantasy and are associated only with such names as that of Count St. Germaine and C. R. C., the illustrious head of the Rosicrucian Mystery School. However, these things are perfectly possible of attainment by all those who are willing to pay the price which this development entails. It means the renunciation of "things" and complete dedication of spirit. The Christ made this truth plain when He said, "My kingdom is not of this world," and again, "My sheep know my voice and follow me."

From this amalgamation of the four Elements a new and fifth Element is formed. As we come into ever increasing attunement with the incoming Aquarian Age, space travelers of the future will be able to contact this new Element and many of the glorious wonders which it will reveal. Perhaps the best description of it is given by St. John in his Revelation, wherein he describes it as a "sea of glass." Upon this sea of glass, he asserts, will be gathered the redeemed and regenerated of all mankind.

Ancient Masters of Wisdom foretold the discovery of this new Element. Some called it Azoth, others termed it Rebis. Both are five-lettered words, or mantrams of power, and both mean the consummation of all things. Hence it will be noted that this new Element typifies the Spirit of Oneness. Before man is worthy to explore its wonders, the world must have come into realization of the Fatherhood of God and the Brotherhood of Man.

The Sixth, Seventh, Eighth and Ninth of the Lesser Mysteries deal with still higher and more exalted spiritual attainment. In the Ninth Mystery the participant passes into the heart of the earth, there to stand in the presence of the Lord Christ to be prepared by Him for the still higher work of the first of the Greater Mysteries.

The most priceless of all Christ's gifts to this earth was the Four Greater or Christ Mysteries, thus making thirteen in all, outlining the Path of complete emancipation under the Christ regime.

The first of the Greater Christ Mysteries will take man to the end of this Earth Day Manifestation. It is here that the Initiate exchanges his Initiate Body for the Body of Adeptship. He now discovers the power of the Lost Word, and possesses the ability to speak all things into creation. Every thought may now be clothed in form at will. Such an illustrious one has now passed beyond the alternation of life and death. This was the sublime attainment of the beloved St. John, the most advanced of all the disciples and the only one who did not pass through the interlude called death.

The powers developed in the first of the Greater Mysteries were demonstrated by the disciples on the day of Pentecost. It was then that they experienced their first intimate communion with the exalted Being known as the Holy Spirit. By the spiritual force now awakened within them they manifested many of the same powers which the Christ exercised during His earthly ministry. These are but some of the extraordinary powers awaiting man when he is found worthy to enter into the first of the Greater Christ Mysteries.

The First Symphony and the First Mystery are under the direction of the Hierarchy of Pisces, the Master Adepts, or perfected humanity.

The Second Symphony and the Second Mystery are under the jurisdiction of the Hierarchy of Aquarius, the Angels.

The Third Symphony and the Third Mystery are under the guidance of the Hierarchy of Capricorn, the Archangels.

The Fourth Symphony and the Fourth Mystery are under the direction of the Hierarchy of Sagittarius, the Lords of Mind.

The Fifth Symphony and the Fifth Mystery are under the supervision of Scorpio, the Lords of Form.

The Sixth Symphony and the Sixth Mystery are under the jurisdiction of Libra, the Lords of Individuality.

The Seventh Symphony and the Seventh Mystery are under the influence of the Hierarchy of Virgo, the Sons of Wisdom.

The Eighth Symphony and the Eighth Mystery are under the guidance of the Hierarchy of Leo, the Lords of Love and Light.

The Ninth Symphony and the Ninth Mystery are under the supervision of the Hierarchy of Cancer, the Cherubim.

There is an intimate relationship between the Ninth of the Lesser Mysteries and the First of the Greater Christ Initiations. The triumphant chorusing of the Cherubim form a musical bridge between the two. It is here that one comes to stand before the sacred secret of Life itself.

The first of the Greater Christ Initiations is under the guidance of the Hierarchy of Gemini, the Seraphim. The keynote of Gemini is Polarity and the keynote of the First Great Initiation is also Polarity. It is here that the Initiate body is exchanged for the body of Adeptship, which means the perfectly polarized, or androgynous body.

The second of the Greater Christ Initiations is under the guidance and direction of the Hierarchy of Taurus, the Teraphim.

The third of the Greater Christ Initiations is under the guidance of Aries, the Xeophim.

It is in the fourth and last of the Greater Christ Initiations that the entire twelve of the Zodiacal Hierarchies pour forth their magic and their power. It is here that the great celestial choir sounds forth in a mighty paen of glory. Such triumphant chorusing as no human ears can hear — nor is it possible for human language to begin to describe its sublimity. We can only say that in this far distant time the Lord Christ Himself is the perfect type pattern of the perfected race which shall come to this exalted place of experience. For man shall then have become Christed, and the dream of St. Paul realized when he said, "Let the Christ be formed in you." This will mark the termination of the Christ Dispensation of earth, and He will return the Kingdom to the Father. Then will a perfected humanity be ready for a still more spiritual teaching which will be the Religion of God the Father.

Part I of this volume deals with music in relation to human evolution. It endeavors to set forth how, by the power and magic of this highest of all arts, man became man. In the far distant future, by the means of this same musical power and magic, man will become more than man; he will become a God-man.

The high spiritual keynote that is resounding through all creation, which Beethoven made articulate in his incomparable creations, is "Onward and Upward Forever."

Other Works by the Same Author

OLD TESTAMENT VOL. I — The Hexateuch .
OLD TESTAMENT VOL. II — Part I — Solomon
and the Temple Buillders. Part II — Books of
Initiation .
OLD TESTAMENT VOL. III — Part I — The
Promise. Part II — The Preparation .
NEW TESTAMENT VOL. IV.
NEW TESTAMENT VOL. V.
NEW TESTAMENT VOL. VI.
THE MYSTERY OF THE CHRISTOS .
HOLY EASTER MYSTERIES .
HOLY CHRISTMAS MYSTERIES .
HEALING MIRACLES OF CHRIST JESUS .
QUESTIONS AND ANSWERS ON BIBLICAL ENIGMAS .
BIBLE AND THE STARS .
NUMBERS AND THE BIBLE .
OCCULT ANATOMY AND THE BIBLE. Series of 12
brochures .
MYTHOLOGY AND THE BIBLE .
THE MYSTERIES OF THE HOLY GRAIL .
ESOTERIC MUSIC Based on the Musical Seership of
Richard Wagner .
BEETHOVEN'S NINE SYMPHONIES Correlated with the
Nine Spiritual Mysteries .
AMERICA'S INVISIBLE GUIDANCE .
HEALING AND DISEASE In the Light of Rebirth
and the Stars .
HEALING AND REGENERATION THROUGH
MUSIC .
HEALING AND REGENERATION THROUGH COLOR .
THROUGH THE YEAR WITH MARY .
SUPREME INITIATIONS OF THE BLESSED VIRGIN .
LENTEN PEARLS .
MYSTIC MASONRY—Five brochures: 1, Esoteric Architec-
ture; 2, The Journey Toward the East; 3, Ascending
Jacob's Ladder; 4, Masonry and the Bible; 5, Man: The
Temple of the Living God.

BEETHOVEN'S NINE SYMPHONIES
Correlated with the Nine Spiritual Mysteries

Beethoven was one of the most important evangels of the New Age that ever came to earth. Every one of his magnificent musical compositions sounds the note of freedom, emancipation, equality and the eventual and permanent conquest of good over evil.

This book is a revealing study of the mystical import of these famous symphonies.

Beethoven has translated for human hearing the celestial music associated with the nine major steps in the initiatory process.

Mrs. Heline's keen insight into the relationship of music to the path of self mastery and conscious evolution is brilliantly told in these pages.

Corinne Heline

Born to the aristocracy of the Old South into the prominent Duke family, she received a classical and religious education that was to prepare her for her life work. She was a life-long student of the ancient mysteries devoting her time to study and meditation. The Rosicrucian adept, Max Heindel, became her teacher and associate at Mt. Ecclesia in Oceanside, California where she met another New Age pioneer, Theodore Heline who was to become her husband and to undertake the publication of the inspired writings that flowed through her. Her monumental work, *The New Age Bible Interpretation,* in 7 volumes was followed by many other works interpreting the ancient wisdom in terms of the needs of the day. She was truly a New Age Pioneer, opening the way to vast new fields of investigation for those who would know and be a part of the coming world of the Aquarian Age. Her consciousness far transcended that of her day, and while she had physical plane teachers, her inspiration came from the immortals who overshadowed her, the greatest being our lovely lady, the Madonna who was the light of her life from early childhood.